BA to BOARDROOM
With No BS,
SKILLS FOR LIFE

BY CHRISTOPHER WILSON

BANKING WITH
NO B.S.

NB Needham Bank℠

MEMBER FDIC | MEMBER SIF | ⌂

D1372764

THE

Copyright © 2013 by Christopher Wilson

BA to Boardroom With No BS, Skills for Life
By Christopher Wilson
www.batoboardroom.com

13-ISBN: 978-0-9851901-4-9
10-ISBN: 0985190140

Library of Congress Control Number: 2013910686

1. Leadership

2. Career development

3. College graduates—Employment

4. Personal motivation—Psychology

5. Team building—Management

6. Executive management

7. Self-help techniques

Edited by: Jennifer Powell
Designed by: Debbi Stocco
Published by: The Missing Peace, LLC

ORDERING INFORMATION:
Quantity discounts are available for bulk purchases by Universities/ Colleges, Career Development Offices, Corporate Training and Human Resource Departments.
Please contact: Chris@batoboardroom.com

Some of the many ideas to explore further in this book:

- ✓ "Knowledge is the mastery of facts. Skill is the mastery of behavior."

- ✓ "Like any learning opportunity, there is a process you can apply to become better at each skill. "

- ✓ "It is no longer about what you are being taught; it is about how fast you can learn."

- ✓ "Not knowing your passion as you graduate is a challenge to be solved, and it isn't done through waiting for an epiphany. It is built through small steps, reflection, taking action and constant effort."

- ✓ "The key purpose of a resume is to get you an interview, not a job."

- ✓ "...don't get caught in the quicksand of wanting to be 100% sure it is the right field."

- ✓ "Management, by definition, means you will succeed through other people."

- ✓ "Listening is different than waiting to speak."

- ✓ "When contemplating a change, be sure you are going TO a new role not AWAY from your current role...Good life advice as well actually."

- ✓ "Times of crises are not times to create a plan, they are times to execute a plan."

- ✓ "Being able to disagree, without being disagreeable is a valuable trait."

SELECTED ENDORSEMENTS

"One of the biggest challenges for career management today is answered in Chris Wilson's book. He successfully guides us on a path of stories, tools and principles that can change our attitudes, alter our behaviors and lead to incredible outcomes. Regardless of career tenure, this book offers real value in our challenging and dynamic workplace today."

Fred M. Studley, Founder of Transition Solutions, providing international career services to corporations for over 25 years.

"This is a poignant and pragmatic book that delivers actionable items delivered with a real world perspective."

Eric Morse, former Global Chief Marketing Officer, CIBC World Markets

---

"This is one of those essential life guides that everyone should have, not to sit on the (actual and virtual) bookshelf, but to return to over and over. How to think through life's choices, how to remember what matters, how to ask the right questions, and how to say what needs to be said. All told in an engaging and conversational style, Wilson has been there and has observed others do it right and wrong. A perfect gift from parents to young people as they start out in their careers, but they might have trouble actually handing it over once they start reading it themselves—so best to buy two copies! This is really for anybody who wants to think carefully about how to take charge of life's transitions."

Paul F. Levy, former CEO, Beth Israel Deaconess Medical Center and author of *Goal Play! Leadership Lessons from the Soccer Field.*

For a complete listing of endorsements, visit www.batoboardroom.com

ACKNOWLEDGEMENTS

I believe in the idea that acquiring skills can produce equal or better results than having technical knowledge alone. The understanding began with many ideas discussed over hours spent talking with my grandparents, Eugene "Bill" Wilson and Louise Wilson. They openly shared their life experiences and guiding principles that helped me shape the foundation of the ideas presented in this book. Over the years, I have had the pleasure of being a mentor, coach, parent or friend to many people who were seeking ways to improve their ability to succeed at their chosen profession. Every time I worked with someone on personal or professional improvement he or she would say, "You should write a book." So I have decided to heed that request and produce a book that I hope will help whomever chooses to read it lead a more rich and positive life.

This book would not have been written without the encouragement of my wonderful wife, Terry. When we met in 2009 she opened many new windows on life for me and is my daily inspiration. Her words and intelligence give me comfort, strength and perspective. She is a treasure and a blessing to me every day. To you my LOML - every day, and in every way, I am proud to be your husband.

Finding ways to clarify your thinking is one of life's challenges and nothing brings greater clarity than being a parent. My two daughters, Curry and Talcott, have kept me focused on what is important in life and parenting daughters as a father requires personal growth. Thank you both, and each, for bringing richness to my life beyond anything I could have imagined. I am extremely proud of you. It is an honor to say I'm your father. I love you each the most.

To the thousands of people I have been fortunate enough to work with, each of you has helped me hone the skills discussed on these pages. Like all of life's relationships, some people have contributed by showing me how to use skills and others by how not to use them. Each experience has value and learning from every personality style one comes in contact with is important to personal growth.

It would not be possible to name everyone involved, as I would inevitably leave someone out. To all my senior management teams, there was no greater pleasure than working with you. To all my peers and bosses, thank you for teaching me in your own individual way. To all the people who worked in my divisions and companies, I am forever grateful for your efforts to drive our success and I hope you look back on our days together with the same fondness I do.

To my publisher, The Missing Peace, LLC...okay it's my wife and me...this has been an adventure and I think technically we have now published a trilogy of unrelated books. The first was *Waking Up: Climbing through the Darkness*, by Terry Wise, and the second was *Viewer Indiscretion*, by T.L. Wilson. Both are great books for very different reasons. Thanks also go to my editor, Jennifer Powell, who challenged my thinking (and sentence structure) in valuable ways and made this a much better piece of work.

And finally, thank you to all the people I am lucky enough to call friends. You add the depth and width to life and I am always amazed at how full life is because of each of you.

Table of Contents

How to Use This Book and Skills Inventory

BA to Boardroom is designed to be a reference tool for you as you move through your career and life. It provides invaluable information for those entering the workforce; either as a college student or a person transitioning back in after time away. It is also a great resource for people taking on greater management and leadership roles. This book features an array of personal and professional skills. They are identified through personal stories that illustrate how they were applied in actual situations.

The discussion of skills is expanded at the end of chapters to give you enough detail to begin working on using the skill effectively. You can choose to skip over skills you don't need at the moment. Chances are as you move through your career, you will find that you need certain skills and the approach used here can change with you as your career changes. There are personal skills, management skills and leadership skills along with insights on career related topics. The idea is for you to have them all in one place rather than searching through multiple books or articles.

Developing these skills will not lead everyone to the boardroom nor is that even an aspiration for many people. If you choose to work on building these skills, you will become more successful in your career regardless of the field you choose or the level you aspire to. As an added benefit, when consistently applied, they will help you in your life outside of work as well.

Index of Skills

Individual Skills

Management Skills

Leadership Skills

Insights

Life Skills

CHAPTER 1

A Matter of Degree

Knowledge is the mastery of facts.
Skill is the mastery of behavior.

inally, after all those classes, papers and stressful exams, there it was in my hand, a BA in History, Lake Forest College, 1979. "Now what?" I thought. I had no classes scheduled, my dorm room was vacated and all my possessions were in the car. Summer break and next year's classes were vestiges of the past. I had no plan beyond leaving. Amidst all the congratulations and cheerful faces, I was nervous about what the future would hold and what I would do to get started. The reality that I was now on my own was here, staring me in the face.

Had someone come up then and offered a lifetime employment contract at $20,000 a year I would have signed it on the spot. If anyone then told me that my career would include being CEO of a financial services company with over $1 billion in revenue, affecting the lives of thousands of employees and earning seven figures followed by becoming a board director in the energy field, I would have laughed. The last math class I took was Algebra 2 in sophomore year of high school and I barely got by that with a D. All that I knew about energy was that it was something you either had in the morning or you didn't.

But this is a true story. From that day with BA in hand, I have made a series of decisions—some small, others large—over 34 years that took me on a path I never could have imagined. What I learned is that the accumulation of skills, not just knowledge, opened many doors and built strong relationships in my work and personal life. Skills in areas such as job search basics, personal improvement, teamwork, strategy, management and leadership all make a difference.

"What are you doing after College?"

Isn't that a great question? It is the last of the trilogy of college-related questions, the first two of course being, "Where are you going to school?" and "What's your major?" The problem for me was that I really didn't have a good answer. I wasn't really sure what I was qualified to do. After all, what kind of a professional career can you build on a collection of jobs that included being a short order cook, shoveling horse stalls at a Christian dude ranch, selling knife sets door to door, working in a gas station, seal coating driveways and filling potholes for the Highway Department? Yes all these jobs, and a few more, put cash in my pocket for spending money during college but they did not seem to prepare me for life after school. I was certainly in trouble, or so I thought at the time.

Getting your college degree is a significant accomplishment and you should take pride in that. School has been a source of structure—class times, activities, housing and meals. While it has given you a measure of independence, you now completely control the outcomes in your life. Making your own choices will replace having some choices made for you. You can do it and will do it many times over your lifetime.

So what do you have to offer as a newly minted, or soon to be, college graduate? Plenty. You already have a range of skills that were not on your tests, were not lectured about and are probably not ones you give yourself credit for as you start to build a life. These skills and others, when recognized, studied and applied will become equally, possibly even more, important than the knowledge you have retained. They are transferable between career fields so investing time to become competent will be something to take with you as you move through new parts of your life.

Some graduates are fortunate to have identified a passion for a certain field and have a clear plan to pursue that passion, but many have not found theirs yet. Not knowing your passion as you graduate is a challenge to be solved, and it isn't done through waiting for an epiphany. It is built through small steps, reflection, taking action and constant effort.

While it does happen that some people find accelerated success in a field and the associated rewards, most successful careers are built over a length of time, not at a moment in time. These career stories are not the ones that make instant news in today's sensationalist media. Building your career requires setting goals for yourself, understanding the steps you need to achieve them and then making good decisions and applying yourself fully to that pursuit.

Opportunity and luck will be factors in many choices you face. To put yourself in the best position to take advantage of these factors, you need to have skills to apply to the situation. For example, your first job may have nothing to do with your long-term career outcome, but you need to grab an opportunity to gain experience.

There will be times in your career where progress seems slow and other times where choices are abundant and you are faced with multiple good options. Keeping an open mind, maintaining awareness and knowing how to make good decisions will produce better outcomes.

When you look back after two or three decades of work, you will be able to reflect on your choices. During your career, the most important action to take is to make choices. One of my favorite quotes is by Yogi Berra, "When you come to a fork in the road, take it." The point is you need to start by actually making a choice, then making it the "right" choice. When you are faced with times that have a number of good choices for different reasons, it is important that you choose one and fully apply yourself to making it the best choice.

All of my choices, not any single choice, led to my becoming a CEO of various companies. The knowledge needed to perform those jobs was vast and was accumulated over many years. Knowledge can be rapidly learned in so many ways today—search engines, on-line courses, job training—and I would encourage you to pursue gaining knowledge with the same energy you did when you worked for your favorite professor. You will certainly need to increase your competency in your field to advance but there is an equal need to become more skillful.

Setting Yourself Up for Success

The goal of this book is to show you how fundamental skills are to all that you do to help you motivate yourself to work on them. Many people are brilliant in their field but deficient in their skills and, as a result, miss achieving the results they want. Having a strong intellect does not guarantee that a person has the ability to apply that talent to a given field. By working on skill sets, you will gain greater self-awareness about what you do and build a structure to manage your life more effectively.

The great thing about skills is that they are transferable. You can use them in your job or in your personal life as you manage the outcomes you hope to achieve. Building on the skills you have already discovered in life, and NEVER stopping the push to achieve greater competency in them, will drive your success.

Like any learning opportunity, there is a process you can apply to become better at each skill. It is important to start with becoming aware that there is a skill to be worked on.

So how do you actually acquire and use skills? The chart on the next page shows you what the skill building process looks like. Start in the lower left box.

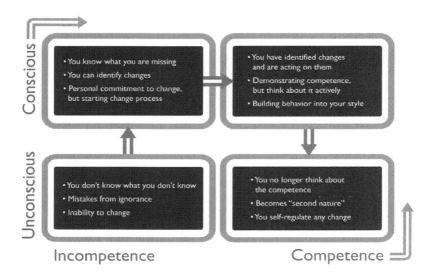

You are not born with complete knowledge and that is why it is important to continue learning throughout your life. Like any new capability, you will get better as you use skills more and be able to grow at a more rapid rate.

Let's take a look at this process in more detail.

At first, you are unaware of the need to work on a skill until it is identified. In other words, you don't know what you don't know. This is not a critique at all; it's simply a truth. This is known as being "unconsciously incompetent" and change is not possible without awareness. Think of the first time you were introduced to a new skill—maybe a new sport or a new summer job skill. You had to be told that the skill actually existed before you could even think about using it.

Once you are aware of the skill and you know how to start using it, you will need time and practice to become better at it. In the beginning it may feel uncomfortable or awkward to work on and you have to think about it very actively to begin using it. This is known as being "consciously incompetent." The change process has started. Here, think about the new skill you identified above. Chances are someone helped you understand the basic concepts and showed you how to start using them. Your proficiency was probably limited at the start.

As you practice more, the skill will become easier and a part of your conscious thought. You will become more successful with it and will feel more comfortable. You will begin using the skill instinctively in certain situations. This is known as becoming "consciously competent." Using your example, do you remember that as you gained more confidence through practice, the skill seemed easier?

If you apply the skill regularly and make it part of your personal "fabric" you will not have to review each step each time; you will just do it. The skill becomes part of your personal style. This is known as becoming "unconsciously competent." It may not be effective every time and that should not be your expectation. However, the skill will give you greater chances for success and that is the intent. Outcomes have other variables that differ in each situation. Unconscious competence is referred to, at times, as "becoming second nature."

Think about learning to use a keyboard as a simple example. The first time you saw one you had no idea what it was or how to use it. Soon, someone showed you how it was structured and how to use it. Then, you practiced and became more proficient and became more comfortable with its purpose. Now, chances are you type without thinking about it; you do it "unconsciously."

I have always viewed the accumulation of skills as filling a toolbox. With each new tool, you become more equipped to build a better outcome. Results are achieved through choosing the right tools for the right job. Once you build a full set of tools, choosing the right one will become easier.

CHAPTER 2

Opening Your Toolbox

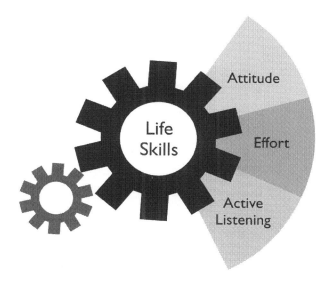

There are personal skills that build a foundation for how you will operate as an adult. These skills are not bestowed upon anyone through a degree. In my case, the important people in my life modeled them.

Eugene "Bill" Wilson, my grandfather, was not a man who pontificated about his success although his accomplishments were extensive. Each day would find Bill dressed in his signature khaki pants and flannel shirt, "whistling on his way to work and whistling coming home," as my grandmother was fond of saying. He was the dean of admissions at Amherst College for 35 years, and one of the most admired men I have ever known.

He looked forward to all aspects of living his life—interviewing prospective students, building a freshman class, mentoring, playing virtually any card or board game, playing pool, fly-fishing and spending time with family and friends.

When I was growing up, we spent hours talking during most summers and holiday seasons. We would go fishing early in the morning on Lake Sunapee in New Hampshire and spend the afternoon playing cards, chess, checkers, cribbage, Yahtzee or any other game we could find. At the end of each day I would set my alarm for 5 a.m., the time Bill said *he* would be ready to go fishing the next morning. I would awake to the ringing clock and Bill's loud snoring. I would race out of bed to get him up. He would open his eyes and calmly say, "I'll be right down; just get the gas, cushions, rods, tackle box and load up the boat." Sounded like a good list at age 10.

Like a happy golden retriever I did just that and waited anxiously in the small boat for his arrival. Normally about 15 minutes later, he appeared in his khakis and flannel shirt, wearing his fishing vest and St. Louis Cardinals hat and off we went. We talked and caught fish for a few hours as the day dawned. When it was time for breakfast, we would go back to the beach where I unloaded the boat and cleaned all the fish, my job he explained, before heading into the house to find Bill reading in his armchair, with a paper and cigar nearby. I loved those times though now I understand it was a form of servitude and he had no intention of being ready by 5 am. He took full advantage of my enthusiasm. Now that I have been a parent, I understand how completely amusing this must have been for him to watch.

Although I didn't realize it at the time, I was learning one of the most important skills I would need from Bill and my grandmother, Lou. They made me feel as if I was the only person in their lives; they were so connected at each point in time. They truly listened, without distraction, to my ideas and thoughts before offering their perspective. The skill they modeled was *active listening* in every conversation and discussion.

Over the years, Bill shared with me other foundational skills. When he assembled the classes of incoming freshmen at the all-male Amherst, he wanted to construct a class of intellectually and culturally diverse, motivated people.

He was a keen judge of character and he took a non-traditional approach to evaluating that at the time. He looked beyond test scores and GPAs and instead defined success more broadly, focusing on a positive attitude and examples of effort in addition to results. He taught me that character is shown through all that you do, not just what is measured in school or on various tests.

Bill would look for examples of these characteristics in a prospective student and then interview him without his family, which was more unique in the 1950s and 60s. Bill's interviews might have been a couple of questions or an hour long, and he would ask enough to validate or disprove what he believed about a candidate's character and the skills he possessed. The result was that some of the students he admitted might not have appeared to be the best on paper. In fact, I've run into a number of successful alumni over my career who have told me, "I have no idea why I was admitted."

I simply smile thinking about Bill's great insights and personal gifts. But his gift to me was to instill the notion that the world was open to more than just the "smartest" people as measured on paper or by tests. There is no one definition of, or model for success. He believed, as I do now, that success is not built from a single element but instead it is identified by motivation, desire and character.

He also showed me that successful decisions are not always the most popular ones. Bill made decisions in his life that were contrary to the popular opinion when he believed strongly about an issue. Some of these were admitting more diverse candidates in the 1950s, pushing for coeducation in the 70s, or being a conscientious objector to the war and spending time in an objector's camp as a result. Being able to disagree, without being disagreeable is a trait he modeled.

Bill sowed many seeds during those memorable years that have fueled my work in understanding the power of building skills. Bill passed away over 30 years ago and I still think about him and his gifts to me and so many others all of the time.

The three skills I learned from Bill, active listening, displaying a positive attitude and putting forth your best effort, serve as a good foundation for adult life. To get a sense of how to use them now, answer the following questions, quietly if you prefer:

1. Do you actively listen to what someone else is saying to you, or do you simply wait to speak?

2. Do you view daily events in your life with a positive attitude regardless of their actual outcome?

3. How self-aware and honest with yourself are you? Do you know when you have applied your best effort to a task and when you have made excuses for not doing so?

Actively listening, building a conscious awareness of the need for a positive attitude and applying your best efforts create a foundation for your life that becomes the compass that leads you down a positive path. They can also help you to navigate the negative outcomes that are a part of everyone's life.

Let's explore each one in more detail.

A Positive Approach

You should not expect to be "happy" all the time or to never express your frustrations. But you can approach all situations and individuals in a positive way in order to see positive results. Simple manners and respect can get you many desired outcomes in life. Think about the person with whom you are interacting and make an effort to figure out what you can do or say that would make that person want to work with you. Are you encouraging and supportive? One way to begin use of this skill is to start your thoughts and actions with:

I will......
I can........
I could........

Rather than

I can't because......
It isn't my issue......
I won't.......

In my own life, I have been fired, divorced and sued. These sound horrible and believe me, not one of those events was pleasant. They did not, however, "ruin my life." They were situations that required resolution and I approached each one in the most positive way I could. Even negative or difficult situations become better when you put your thinking and actions in a positive framework. In my case, I was rehired and am now extremely happily married because I refused to let the negative outcomes snowball into a negative attitude. In fact, the adversity produced much better outcomes for me long term.

The Life Events chart below illustrates a range of events that you might encounter in your own life. Typically, people would conclude that only the positive outcome boxes (the two on the right) are the ones where you can feel good about yourself, but that is not true.

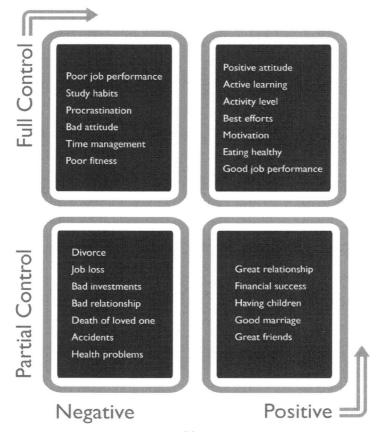

You do have a choice, every time, whether you fully control the outcome or not.

This does not mean that a negative outcome will be easier, but a positive approach will help you weather the storm better. While you may have to accept an outcome, you are the person responsible for pleasing yourself and judging yourself.

Rather than work to be positive, some people find it easier to assign blame to something or someone and not reflect and learn from their own mistakes. Wisdom comes from years of honest self-reflection and the ability to learn from your findings. Therapists make a great living by helping people understand these issues. So if you are not planning on being a therapist, or cannot afford one, take time to reflect on how you approach your own life. Write down what you think about—unfiltered. Then go back and decide if you need to change your approach to be more positive. If so, make a commitment to yourself to apply needed changes.

Applying Yourself

The second skill, *best effort,* requires personal honesty and accountability. It is hard to view what you do objectively and most of us would prefer to rationalize our behavior rather than face our shortcomings. But you cannot fix something unless you first acknowledge it needs fixing. We all know when we have applied our best effort but rarely are we honest enough with ourselves to be truly self-accountable. As you move into adult life, you need this ability as people around you are unlikely to remind you of your areas for improvement or they do so in an unkind way. The more honest you are with yourself, the more motivational and powerful this skill becomes to drive change.

The reality is that it is a high standard personally, but it enables you to survive many changes in your life that are not your choice. Knowing you were honest, ethical and hard working is enough to declare success, even when others may view it differently. The reality is it is difficult to call something a failure if you have truly given it your best. Thomas Edison referred to his unsuccessful inventions as finding many ways that things didn't work, not as failures. Countless other successful people have pointed out that trying new approaches is simply part of finding success, not promoting failure. The outcome may not be what was desired, the rewards may have been missed, but if you can honestly say you have put forth your best effort, you know the outcome was the result of the best you could do.

Listening, not waiting to speak

Active listening is the one skill that is in shortest supply in the world today. Ironically, it is also a skill that would greatly improve people's lives. There is great value in telling people that we understand what they are saying.

Active listening is critical to your success. It builds connection. Everyone wants to be heard and appreciated. Taking time to understand someone else's viewpoint—even if you disagree—makes them feel valued. People who feel valued are more likely to work with you towards a successful outcome whether at work or home. They are also more likely to listen to you.

Active listening also creates a common understanding and definition of an issue. Many times people assume they are operating from a common definition of an issue but, because people's perspectives may be different, they never reach alignment of that definition. Active listening says to the other person, "I want to know what you mean." As you ask questions and listen to responses, you can begin to match up where you agree and where you don't.

Finally, active listening ultimately saves time in decision making. Once you truly understand the person's perspective, you will be able to say, "I think we can agree on 80% of the issues here." You can then outline them, get agreement and move to the remaining open items. You will be amazed at how much more you will accomplish and how positive people will feel about dealing with you.

Listening is different than waiting to speak. Rather than formulating your own thoughts while someone else is talking, look at them and listen to their words and tone. Stephen Covey called this concept "Seek first to understand, then be understood" and it is a sound practice. Some people who do not invest the time to actively listen rely on advocacy and a louder voice to get what they want. These choices create greater risks, such as relationship breakdowns, unconstructive dialogue and wasted time. Try confirming your understanding of what someone is saying to you when working through an issue in the future. Reflect back to them what you heard and confirm that your understanding is correct. You will see a difference in the dialogue.

To the extent that these three skills are not part of your approach to life, commit to begin trying them. That is different than getting it right every time. Remember the learning process, apply it consistently and you will see the changes.

Learning is a lifelong process. Whether you are learning about a career, learning to parent, pursuing a hobby or learning how to improve personally, you will ALWAYS be learning and should enjoy the ride! It is not an optional exercise. Learning is required in today's world.

CHAPTER 3

Taking Inventory & Making Choices

S kills are introduced early in your life even if they are not recognized immediately. For example, summer jobs in the teens begin to add skill basics to your toolbox.

At age 15, I took a job as a snack bar cook at the Rhode Island Country Club pool. I flipped burgers, poured Cokes and cleaned my shack every day. I got to know the members and formed new relationships as I learned how to do this job. While one skill I got was the ability to make a great hamburger, I also learned about the importance of positive customer relations, how to take criticism (poorly cooked burger) and how to respond to it, how to manage time and how to work for a boss.

The next summer, I went to Colorado from Boston. There were no cell phones, no job, no Internet and no friends. I lived in a firehouse outside Denver for two weeks before finding a job at a dude ranch in southern Colorado. I hopped a bus there and walked down the long dirt driveway. When I arrived, I immediately had my shoulder length blond hair cut off. That was my first lesson in conforming to the requirements for a job. We are not always presented with requirements with which we agree.

My tasks were to learn how to shovel out horse stalls by day and wash dishes at night. After three days living in a bunkhouse and working in less than optimal conditions, I packed my backpack and snuck out at 3 am, walking 6 miles down dark roads to find the bus station and grabbed the first bus going as far away as the $5.40 in my pocket would take me. From this job, I learned that I didn't ever want to own a horse. I also learned a basic decision-making skill: take action, rather than wait for someone else to do it.

The bus took me to a small mountain town where I made a collect call to my parents (yes through an operator) and asked if they would pay for a room for two nights at a local motel while I looked for work. They did and I promptly went to the room, shut the door and cried.

Eventually, I picked myself up and found work at a local gas station working the "graveyard shift." I acquired great customer service and sales skills from a surprisingly astute station owner and learned how to build my own life—get an apartment, shop, pay rent and budget. I went back for the next two summers and built a life and friends in that small town. I opened the gift of independence.

Another summer produced a job through a family friend shoveling asphalt into potholes on the streets of St. Louis, possibly the most humid place in America in the summer. The first day I walked into the highway department, it quickly became clear I was the only person attending school much less college and I was met with a measure of disdain. In fact, I felt as if I would not live through the day given the looks I received. The day began and I hopped up in a dump truck sitting between Ben and George, whom I suspected were headed for death row. They were my summer partners and I spent my non-riding time for the next eight weeks walking behind that dump truck for 5-7 miles a day while Ben drove, shoveling out 400 degree Fahrenheit asphalt and putting it in various size holes in the roads. I learned what I did not want to do for a career and that hydration is critical to survival in extreme heat. I also learned how to work with people who have completely different backgrounds and viewpoints, how to communicate and be part of a team.

Back at school, I started a small business with a friend seal coating driveways in the affluent suburbs of Chicago. It was so profitable that two of us worked one day a week (and two days making bids) and cleared $2,500 a week. Twenty-five dollars worth of materials and two to three hours of work were worth $1,000 to 2,000 per driveway. I learned about profit margins, marketing, competitive selling, perceived value and satisfying customers.

There were other jobs, but the point is that even the seemingly low level job or a job you dislike can give you skills to build on. Take your inventory and see what you have already. My guess is you have a number of skill basics you can build on.

Your educational background is worth reviewing for how it has created a foundation of skills for you.

With my BA in hand, I searched for the concrete definition that enabled me to say, "This is what I did in college"—at least on the surface. Some majors leave you struggling to determine how to apply your knowledge to a career. I would ask you to think about the skills *you have*, rather than those you have not, acquired.

- Did you learn to think through issues by researching various viewpoints?

- Did your classes involve challenging and/or defending your hypotheses?

- Did you learn how to communicate through the written and spoken word more effectively?

- Did you learn about teamwork through your studies or outside activities?

- Did you learn about leadership through sports or other non-classroom activities?

- Were you encouraged to work on relationship skills through your nights and evening?

While all of these answers are probably, "Well yeah, of course," surprisingly all of these create foundational skills for success in your career and life that can be advanced through thoughtful learning, thinking and application. Think of building a stronger set of skills the same as if you as were pursuing a master's degree, only your life is the classroom. The successful path from BA to Boardroom is traveled using skills you already have but may not realize it, coupled with learning and applying additional skills.

So, you already have the following skills through your education:

- Critical Thought
- Rapid Learning
- Research Techniques
- Basic Team Dynamics
- Relationship Building
- Writing and Making Presentations

From the base you already have, you can now begin to add skills that appeared as I navigated my career that can help you in your career and adult life. Where appropriate in these next chapters, I will also share some insights and ways to make choices that may be helpful to you. Business stories are used to illustrate how these skills were applied to actual situations because that is how I identified them. *However, these are not just skills for business; they are skills for life.*

As you approach any challenge, it is normal to be nervous when life is about to change significantly from what you have known. You are now responsible for your own successes, your own structure, your own achievements and your own assessment. You can do it, not always in one great leap, but by continuing to learn how to build the skills needed to succeed.

I did not believe that about myself at age 22, but I absolutely believe it now.

Making Choices

We still haven't addressed the seemingly endless choices you now have as you prepare to start your career: where to live, how to find a field you enjoy and how to move forward in your career.

Deciding where to live partly depends on your personal preferences. You can always choose to live where you grew up. If at all possible, try to avoid being a baby boomer-ang living at home. There are sometimes economic realities that require it, but keep the time as short as possible as this only delays the inevitable journey into adult life.

Another way to approach the question is to look at what parts of the world, not just the country, have jobs in your desired field. Do not make excuses such as "I don't know anybody" or "It's so far away." They will keep you from evaluating your full range of options. You are in the first generation of truly global citizens. Yours is a generation that takes your entire life with you. Facebook friends, and their friends, are always a click or text away. You can Skype from almost anywhere and attend a party on the other side of the world if your friend has Wi-Fi. So acknowledge to yourself when you are making excuses and go build your life. Mobility is an advantage in today's world if you choose to use it.

Choosing a career field is a pursuit where you need to invest some time. Chances are you have already done so but if not, don't get caught in the quicksand of wanting to be 100% sure it is the right field. In today's workforce, the average person will change fields over half a dozen times. What is important is to think about your interests and look at the macro world around you for a field that offers enough growth potential to support a multi-year career.

You went through a similar decision-making process before when you chose a school. You had to develop criteria that were important to you and make a decision based on those criteria. This is the same process with different criteria. You can do it just as you have before.

Jobs vary in content but have some common characteristics. Looking at what characteristics feel best to you will help you select a role that can produce the highest likelihood of being one in which you feel comfortable. Here are a few questions to help you focus on what job characteristics might work best for you. When you decide what works best for you, you can narrow your search by eliminating jobs that have characteristics that do not appeal to you.

- Does the job involve dealing with people more than doing just your own work? Sales, service, travel, phone work, retail, food and beverage and hospitality are potential fields of employment that involve interacting with people. These types of jobs tend to have lots of change on a regular basis versus a list of tasks to complete.

- Does the job involve more scheduled activity, tasks and definable outcomes? Legal, administrative, operations, technology, finance and others are potential good fits. These jobs fit best for people who like to work independently.

- Is the job an individual contributor role or part of a team? Are you more comfortable in one type of job than the other? Would you rather be self-directed?

- What level of definition do you need to do work? Larger companies tend to have more structure and smaller ones may require you to be more self-directed.

Picking the criteria that are right for you will help create a filter as you look at different options. Be honest with yourself and pick the path you want or will enjoy most, not what others want. There are no right answers here, just what works for you. Remember, you may not get everything you want with your first job, but asking yourself these questions can help guide you as you advance through your life and career.

Choosing a field seems like a daunting task when you are first starting out. It becomes less daunting if you study your choices and understand what is important for you. There are always reasons why "not" to do something and you will always have people who tell you what you should do. You need to gather information from people you trust, document it (yes, writing it down helps) and then make your own choice. Many people feel obligated to follow their parents' wishes or to heed one person's advice above their own viewpoint. Don't.

The great news about being an adult is that you need to be sure you are making choices that work best for you, not for others. This does not mean turn into a selfish narcissist; it does mean that you are the only one who can determine what is best for you because you have to live with yourself. It's very liberating when you embrace the concept.

In choosing a career, there is no one path to follow. If you are fortunate enough to have a passion and a skill to match, go for it. Nothing is more rewarding than having that type of alignment when you start your career. If, on the other hand, you are faced with choosing a path, look at the world around you. Look at trends in society and areas that are growing. They are plentiful. A few examples:

- The energy field—energy production, alternative energy companies and energy efficiency.

- Worldwide trade of retail goods.

- Greater education needs and reforms.

- Growth of on-line commerce is a foundation of life today.

- Financial services for everyday living.

- Data aggregation is a key theme, taking data and turning it into information then knowledge.

- Health Care is booming. Obesity and nutrition need to be addressed.

- Aging of baby boomers and growth of required services.

- Travel and hospitality.

- Scarcity of water will create a whole new industry.

- Public service has significant needs.

All of these trends, and many more, need people to fuel their growth. Do not assume that ALL jobs require knowledge you do not possess; there are many that need your general intelligence, work ethic *and skills*. Expanding industries need both specialists and generalists so you can find employment in any of these fields with a liberal arts background.

Industries change over time, but identifying key trends gives you a perspective that can grow with an industry. One easy example of trend evolution is the drugstore business. In the 70s, most neighborhoods had a local drugstore. In the 80s, forward-thinking business people applied bulk purchasing principals to the industry and the "CVS era" was born. In the 90s retailers like Wal-Mart, Stop & Shop and others challenged the single-themed CVS and put out diversified bulk purchasing businesses, creating significant pricing pressure on local stores. In the 2000s, consumers sought even greater price efficiency and convenience giving rise to companies like Drugstore.com that can deliver products the next day, right to your house.

This is an example of one industry with multiple cyclical evolutions. All cycles were driven by the consumers' needs (not the businesses' desire) for better prices and greater convenience. As an employee, it would have been great to have the specialized knowledge of a pharmacist (ironically, pharmacists roles decreased significantly) but I guarantee there were many more jobs in the drugstore field that did not require that knowledge.

Take some time and identify trends you think are critical to today's world over the next 20-30 years. Try to target a field that will give you some room for advancement simply by growth of the field. Immerse yourself in learning as much as you can about all facets of the field and apply *the skills* you will be accumulating.

What about Grad school?

This is one of the most common questions I get asked by college graduates. The short answer is, if it is a requirement for a specific career choice, do it. If you haven't come up with a better plan and want to just stay in school, don't necessarily do it. Graduate school costs money and it takes time. The costs to you, in addition to tuition, could also include lost wages and experience so be certain you can make up those losses after graduating. The advanced degree may give you better odds of landing a job in your field, but it is not a guarantee.

Keep in mind that you have several options. Advanced study does not have to be a "masters degree or nothing" equation. One of your advantages is that you can learn content based on the skills you have acquired in school. Selectively taking courses needed to add to your knowledge is an option outside a degree program and can be done while you are employed. I added accounting, strategic planning and organizational development to my background through a tuition reimbursement benefit at my work. With the growth of iTunes University, EdX and other online university options, you can build your own advanced knowledge library from the comfort of your own home rather than in the classroom, many times without having to paying a dime. Design your own degree program if you want to study at an advanced level. This is a great way to see whether graduate level study appeals to you as well.

CHAPTER 4

Building a Foundation

n 1980, I made a decision to interview in the business world, even though I hadn't had much exposure to working in a company. The business world seemed to offer the most opportunity at the time and filled the local newspaper with ads for jobs for college graduates. I ventured out to a men's clothing store and splurged on a $99 polyester suit that came with two pairs of pants and a reversible vest. At 6'4" and 151 lbs, I didn't make the suit look much different than it did on the hanger. But when I put on my tan, square-toed Frye cowboy boots and combed my shoulder length hair, I thought I looked pretty good and could now present myself well for a job in business. True story—and took me 30 years to admit I actually did that.

In those days, jobs were mostly local and they were listed every Sunday in a huge section of the local newspaper. I also had friends working in Boston and heard which companies were good places to work and which had less than stellar reputations. One ad in particular caught my eye. It was for Fidelity, at the time a small, not particularly well known mutual fund company. I knew nothing about mutual funds, but the job sounded interesting and Fidelity had an immediate need for people like me. With my resume in hand I proceeded to set up an interview.

The day arrived for my interview at their Boston headquarters. A pleasant human resources recruiter greeted me, asked me basic questions about where I lived, when I could start and if I understood the position. Fortunately, I admitted I didn't and she proceeded to explain the scope of the job.

After a half an hour with her, I was the led to an office where an intimidating supervisor, Linda, was waiting. She was tall and strong and had black hair that didn't move. She was not one for small talk and had an aura of supreme confidence. She barely said hello and started by asking me what I had done in my life that made me think I was qualified for this customer service representative position. As I fumbled my way through my long resume of service positions—short order cook, gas station attendant, door-to-door salesman and highway department worker—she exuded a palpable air of impatience and disdain. She asked about my college career only after mentioning that she never went to college. She never even smiled. I was beginning to wonder whether it was the suit. After grunting, "Thank you for coming in" she sent me on my way.

I had gone in with high hopes, but left with little optimism about being hired. Being anxious to begin earning money, get an apartment and live an independent life I was disappointed. I chalked the interview up to a learning experience.

Much to my surprise, I got home that night to find that Fidelity had called (pre answering machines, computers, internet or cell phones) and left a number for me to call to set up a second interview. The polyester, urban-cowboy, hippie look had worked! I set up the second interview, reversed the vest, donned the other set of pants, put on the boots and went back in to meet Marilyn, the department head and Linda's boss.

Marilyn greeted me warmly with a large smile. She was a smaller woman with a nasal voice who immediately put me at ease. She started by asking how my interview with Linda went.

"Went well I think," I said sheepishly.

"Actually, no it didn't but our HR person thought you'd be great," Marilyn said.

She went on to disclose a little too much about how Linda was not a believer in college graduates from the suburbs. I went with it and had a nervous laugh or two, but I appreciated Marilyn's down-to-earth personality. She then went on to ask very good questions about, of all things, skills. Along the way, she astutely investigated my desire to work with people, how I handled difficult people and how I dealt with stressful situations.

After an hour, she said bluntly, "When can you start?"

I said, "Next week," not even knowing if I was going to get

paid. No one had told me how to negotiate a salary. The pay was $8,500 a year plus overtime. As my fellow workers all joked later, it was a great place to work if your parents could afford to send you there.

"A requirement of working at Fidelity is that we all have to undergo a background check and the first day of work is a company orientation," Marilyn informed me. She picked up the phone, summoned the HR rep and sent me off to complete the background check paperwork and a W-9.

Stunned and thrilled, I spent the rest of the day trying to find a place to live in nearby neighborhoods. As the next week rolled around, I was ready for my first job, had a place to live in town, and I had a clean suit which I soon found out wasn't required.

I showed up Monday morning eager to start, having no idea that this would be the first of 1,563 Monday mornings in my mutual fund career. Orientation covered the company history, benefits and the importance of ethics along with giving me a chance to meet other new employees at Fidelity who were starting that day.

According to my company ID number, I was the 1228th employee hired since they started counting. There were less than 500 people working at the company when I started, and since then, well over 100,000 people have worked there.

The trainer led me down to my department, a single floor with 28 telephone reps (including me), four supervisors (including Linda), and Marilyn. Marilyn greeted me, took me around and introduced me to the supervisors and then showed me my desk. Gulp. I was in Linda's group sitting right behind her desk.

Marilyn wished me luck and said she would be around if I needed anything. I debated taking out the newspaper and looking for another job right then but instead sat down, looked around and waited for Linda to finish a call.

What I came to learn months later, when I was promoted to Linda's peer, was that this was not just a test for me but also a test for her. Marilyn insisted that her supervisors be able to manage all people effectively regardless of whether they "liked" them. This was a great lesson about the requirement for objectivity when you plan to manage people. While Linda did not seem to be in full agreement with the approach, we sat down and she specifically laid out goals, roles and responsibilities. She detailed how I would be measured, what she expected and what my responsibilities were as a customer service telephone rep.

"Don't try to be a hero and make up an answer if you don't know it, Chris, got it? You ask me. Just know I don't like being asked the same question more than once so learn the answers."

While my inside voice was churning on a sly comeback, my external voice said, "Got it Linda."

Learning how to "manage up" to your boss effectively is a critical success factor as well as being a crucial component of career advancement. As I went back to my desk, an older woman one desk away smiled and waved me over. Phyllis, Linda's assistant supervisor, was 20 years older than all of the other reps and simply told me that she would always be available for questions. She said that I should be sure to ask her any question whenever I wanted. I realized then that learning a new role quickly, or rapid learning, requires using all the resources around you and not being shy about saying, "I don't know this."

As the weeks progressed, I learned that I could get answers from many people when I didn't know how to use a system, process a transaction, or deal with a difficult customer. One of the more senior supervisors and Marilyn's "go to" person was Frank who went out of his way to help me get better at what I did, as he did with everyone. He was very patient, skilled at giving feedback, seemed to know everyone and everything, smoked two packs of cigarettes a day at his desk and quickly became someone I grew to respect and admire. Little did I know that 18 years later I would start a company and hire Frank to run operations.

Linda turned into, and remains, a good friend and we get great laughs recounting those early days. To this day she makes it a point to tell me that she wasn't a great fan of mine at the interview. I hope that I played a small part in reducing her bias against people with college degrees. Having now interviewed thousands of people over my career, I now understand how critical it is to make a good first impression when meeting new people, even if you don't share the same perspective.

Resume

Resume is not a French word for Term Paper. It is a critical document that should give someone you don't know enough information to decide you are worth talking to. Write your resume with that in mind.

There are lots of opinions about how to write a good resume and plenty of alternatives. Format matters. Choose one that fits your style. If there is a stack of 100 resumes, it is obvious who doesn't care about how theirs looks. Just like an interview, a date or an important event, if you don't care how you look, why should anyone else?

- The key purpose of a resume is to get you an interview, not a job. Make your resume intrigue the reader enough to bring you in to ask you questions. Give enough information to understand your background, but not so much that they don't need to talk to you.

- Think about the person reading your resume. They are pressed for time and they have multiple resumes to review so every word choice matters.

- Your resume should be succinct, containing few adjectives. Use nouns and verbs and let the interviewer ask you for expanded commentary. Use active verbs to start your description of a task and be sure you keep the verb tense consistent.

- When it comes time to write an objective, take time to think about why you are applying. Your objective should be meaningful, something more than a generic "want a job in business." If you don't have a specific objective, leave it out and explain your intent in your cover letter. You can change the objective to match the job for which you are applying.

- Approach every application and interview as if it were THE job you want. If you were trying out for your favorite play or sports team and said, "Yeah, I guess it would be something I'd like to do," chances are you wouldn't even get an audition much less a part. Make sure your resume and cover letter speak to your desire to get that job.

- Write a professional and direct cover letter to accompany your resume. Use this to show the positive commitment and passion that will get your resume to the top of the pile for an interview.

- Show success. Successful people will succeed again. Highlight the success you have had in school clubs, summer jobs, personal projects or academics. Don't be arrogant, but don't be shy either.

- Highlight your skills and be ready to talk about why they are helpful for the role you want. People can be taught the knowledge, but poor communication and relationship skills can develop into management challenges.

- There is no right answer to, "Does education go first?" on the resume. It is a personal document and you decide based on how YOU want to present your life to someone.

Interview

Here's where the harsh realities of the world come into play. Appearance matters. Show that this interview means something to you. If you have a question about what to wear, dress up a notch. Having interviewed hundreds of people, I can assure you that being neat, standing and sitting tall, making eye contact and shaking hands firmly will make you stand out. We live in a society that some might argue is becoming more superficial, but regardless of your perspective on that, show you care and make a good first impression.

Over the years, I have seen many different approaches. I can generally tell even before we start talking when a candidate is excited about a job. It is clear from the way that candidate presents herself. I appreciate it when the candidate is truly being genuine and relaxed. As an interviewer, you are looking for someone who would be a good fit in your workplace. Since a candidate has no idea what to do to address that need, being genuine enables the interviewer to gauge whether the position would be a good fit for that person's style. This means the candidate also has a higher likelihood of ending up in a place where he or she will be happy.

There is no need to try to compliment the interviewer. It makes us suspicious.

Take a quick look in a mirror prior to coming in. Loose impediments from lunch are uncomfortable to address. I once interviewed a very conservative and nervous middle aged man who was wound up so tightly that he gave only one-word answers. But it wasn't the answers or his hiked up pants or his starched shirt that stood out. It was the toilet paper dragging from his left shoe heel. It reminded me of a bride going down the aisle in a wedding with a long train behind her, but I wasn't sure he would see the humor if I brought it up.

Some other things to keep in mind:

- Be confident and concise. Be human and *pay attention to non-verbal signals* you send off such as sitting with your arms folded on your chest or making no eye contact. Traits like confidence, poise and energy are not spoken but conveyed in the way you present yourself.

- Be prepared. Study as you would for an exam. Know with whom you are interviewing and what the organization does. Use that knowledge in the conversations you have in your interview.

- Actively listen. Ask for clarification when you don't understand a question, don't BS the interviewer. It's okay to say, "I'm not sure I understand the question."

- Don't interrupt.

- Be prepared to articulate your own strengths and areas to improve.

- Be ready to discuss your background.

- Emphasize if are you approachable, flexible and able to work with others.

- Be prepared to explain why someone should hire you over other candidates.

- Be clear in your responses and know when to stop talking. When you focus on really listening to the interviewer, you can stop talking when you have answered a question. The content of your response, not the length, is what matters.

- Do not be afraid of silence between questions. A common tactic of skilled interviewers is to leave dead air between questions to see whether someone rambles. If you have answered the question, wait for the next one.

- Think about what you would want to know if you were the interviewer. Every person interviewing prepares for you as well and they have looked at your information and formulated questions. What would you ask yourself if you objectively looked at your resume? Write down the answers and be prepared to deliver them.

- If you have a sense of humor, it is fine to use it. Sarcasm isn't good, but a funny line (even if pre-planned) about your background works if delivered well.

- Be ready with two or three questions of your own. Others may come out of the interview, but usually you run out of time. Examples:

  "How would you describe a successful candidate for this position?" This allows you to reinforce your job fit to the interviewer.

  "How is success measured at this organization/department?" This gives you insight into whether this is a well-led organization that can clearly define the metrics of success.

- Practice interviewing. You do not want to go into your first interview for the job you really want nervous, unprepared and fumbling. Have answers for common questions about your background or education.

- You may have very few interviews before landing a job or you may have hundreds. The key is to stay patient, be appropriately persistent and approach each interview as if it were your only one. You need to bring the same energy and focus to each interview.

- Avoid using the word "like" multiple times in each sentence, which makes you appear to be a human Facebook page. If you don't know whether you do this, ask your best friend.

- Stay focused. If the interview or the job content turns out to be different than what you thought, consider the interview a practice run for future interviews.

- Some people choose to lead, some to follow and both are critical to an organization's success. Don't assume you do not have skills to contribute.

- Send a follow-up thank-you note. At the very least use email, but sending an additional handwritten note can make a bigger impression

Post-Interview: It is very important to do a couple of activities. Use the contacts folder on your phone and enter the name of each person with whom you spoke. In the notes section add details about them, what you talked about, areas of interest and areas to avoid. You can then refer back to your notes when you next talk and you will present yourself as extremely prepared. Critique what went well and what could have gone better. Keep a list of questions and what you should have said. I still keep notes in this section of my phone to refresh my recollection on my way to meetings.

Negotiating a Salary

This is an area that most people are uncomfortable talking about, but it is important to make sure you understand your pay.

Many times in a first job there is little room for negotiation. Often a position has a pay range and where you fit in that range is dependent on your skills and qualifications. A good employer will have no issue discussing it with you. Questions about how the pay range is established, how increases are decided and the timing of those increases and how job performance is measured are all ways of opening a discussion on pay.

This initial salary can make a big difference in the long run. Generally, your raises will be based on your base pay so it is worthwhile to get the best starting pay possible. Remember, pay includes cash compensation, any incentives and benefits. Benefits have value to you and understanding how you can best use them is important. In some larger organizations, benefits can equate to 20% and more of your total compensation.

If you are changing jobs or negotiating for a second or third job, take some time to review what you are offering the company in terms of experience. Are you going to be one of the more skilled people in your function? Can you point to qualities or experience that sets you apart from the position description for which you are being hired? If so, be sure to point those out in your interview to give as much information as you can to the hiring manager.

The most important part of negotiating a salary is to make sure you "land the job" first before discussing pay. You want the hiring manager to be convinced you are the person they want. Then and only then, initiate the pay discussion. You will be negotiating from a stronger position and the dialogue will have a higher likelihood of producing the best results for you.

- Open the dialogue by asking how the compensation for the position has been set. Was it from market rates? Was it from the pay of the last person in the job? Was it driven by what they could pay? All are starting points for a discussion.

- Understand the larger employment picture to help you make the best choice you can. What is the market for people in this field? What comparable organizations are out there and is the pay competitive?

- Ask if there is room to grow in responsibility and/or pay if you perform well.

Background Checks

An important observation, while not a skill, is that in addition to your resume and the interview, it is common practice to use other assessment criteria. Credit references (know your own credit score), background checks, social media searches and fact-checking of your resume are all standard at many organizations. They are, by definition, invasive and you live in a transparent world. Privacy is rapidly becoming a social artifact. In the age of little privacy, expect to answer questions about the findings.

Because these assessments all help shape the impression you give a potential employer, be painfully honest and complete in the paperwork you submit on your job application. If you have a blemish or transgression, be ready to proactively explain it in a constructive way. Few people in life have no issues to discuss so avoid measuring yourself against perfection. How you recover and explain says a great deal about your character and whether you are a trustworthy person.

For those of you who are more forward thinking, be thoughtful about the electronic image you are creating for yourself; chances are that it will be used to evaluate you in the job process.

An emerging reality for many positions today is there is an increase in drug testing. While my operating assumption is that you have gained enough life wisdom to know that using any sort of banned substance is not a good choice, be aware of the need to verify that with an employer. In companies that operate in multiple states, federal law prevails so do not assume that if you live in a state with more liberal laws that those state laws will protect you, they won't.

Goals, Roles and Expected Results

People always ask, "How do you become a great manager?"

First, managing and leading are distinctly different. In management, you are always being managed as well as managing others. So whether you look up, down or sideways on an organization chart, you are being called on to manage a relationship. Studying management is a lifetime process, but I will give you some core concepts to focus and build on:

- Clarity is the most important concept for managing or being managed. The clearer the definition of the role, the easier it is to perform and measure results.

- In defining the role you are managing, look at the specific tasks required, what time parameters are expected and how you are expected to perform in your role. Spend extra time here, as this definition is critical to accurately measure adequate versus excellent performance.

A few core management skills:

Set goals for performance of the role you are managing. They must be **SMART**: **S**pecific, **M**easureable, **A**ttainable, **R**ealistic and **T**imely.

What are you going to do, by when and how will it be measured (facts)? The goals should be relevant to your work and additive to the goals of your organization. I always asked my teams to give me goals in three categories: company, department and personal. I wanted people to think about how to help the company, how to help their team and also how to personally improve each year.

Measuring results should be easy once you have defined the goals well. In "managing up" to your boss, do not wait for your annual review to update them; give a regular email report or cover progress in your one-on-one meetings. If you are lagging, tell them, don't hide it. Ask for ideas to improve the outcome.

Managing Up

One of the great mistakes new employees make is to believe they should leave their boss alone. However, it is also a mistake to constantly flood your boss with information and appear to be dependent. The balance comes in efficient communication.

- Consider the personality of your boss. Is verbal communication best? Or would a memo work better? Take the time to watch and learn how your boss operates daily. Use the methods of communication that match his or her preferred style.

- Help your boss be successful. Ask if you can do more and ask for feedback periodically. Doing this can benefit you in the long run. Successful bosses get more responsibility and often turn to the people who helped them get there for bigger roles.

- Your boss is being evaluated by how he or she manages you. By excelling at your job and helping him or her achieve their goals, you should both benefit.

- Don't waste your boss's time with idle talk during the workday unless he or she initiates it.

- If you need something, be prepared with your assessment, what you need and the reason for asking.

- If you are struggling with an issue, explain the problem and ask for his or her advice (most bosses also like being a mentor).

- Be concise in measuring results and update him or her periodically on your progress. Some roles have clear metrics; others may need to aggregate data to show progress. A short update ending with, "Let me know if you have any questions," is always appreciated and noticed.

Rapid Learning

The world moves at an increasingly rapid pace. This is a reality you need to fully embrace today. Focus on making it an advantage for you.

When you combine the viral speed of social media avenues with the far-to-wide pipeline of media channels in search of news, new ideas can evolve or be destroyed in minutes. Maintaining expertise in a field over a sustained period of time is challenging. Finding ways to stay current through rapid learning is critical for success. If you have an undergraduate degree, you have an advantage because you know how to learn. However, if you choose to become complacent and not use that skill, you will be left behind by those who do. The tools for doing so become different as you progress in your career.

- It is no longer about what you are being taught; it is about how fast you can learn. Accessing information, digesting key points, finding current updates and allotting time to study are all key behaviors to becoming a rapid learner.

- Starting out in your first job, you need to be self-directed. You have the Internet; you have access to books and industry or trade publications. You can gain access to courses either on-line or locally (in most cases). Look at the field you have chosen and plan time to research and learn, just as you did for your classes. The difference is you have to drive your curriculum, set your class time and hold yourself accountable for doing the work. Be efficient and drive your own learning.

- Take advantage of tuition reimbursement to supplement your learning if your organization offers this benefit.

- Because many people get their first significant career advancement based on their technical knowledge, becoming as well versed in your field as possible can help.

- As you advance, balance growing your skills with maintaining current knowledge. This can become difficult at times. As administrative tasks that do not involve technical knowledge occupy more of your day, your time to maintain your expertise is more limited. You can compensate by hiring people with the needed expertise and creating a team environment where they can succeed. Establishing clear roles and responsibilities and managing the results becomes more critical to success than personally solving each problem based on your own knowledge.

- Success at the top management ranks requires that you manage people with high levels of expertise and maximize their performance. Your ability to rapidly learn what is needed and implement changes will drive your ascent.

CHAPTER 5

Adding New Tools

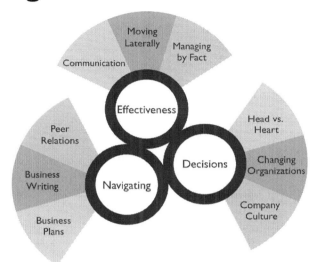

D uring my years at Fidelity, the stock market surge fueled a meteoric rise from $7 billion in assets to over $90 billion. This rapid company growth fueled job growth.

Needs opened in many parts of the company as we grew and I was opportunistic in taking a non-traditional career path. Many people were getting promoted in the same department and becoming more specialized in one aspect of the business. As an alternative, I began to move laterally at a similar salary to gain a broader experience. I decided to build a broad business background following the model of a BA, which gives you a broad background in academics. No doubt my parents assumed I simply couldn't keep my focus, but I was hungry to learn as much as I could during this high-growth period.

Fortunately, there were many needs within Fidelity and opportunities to move. One of the most important things I learned in this fast-paced environment was the need to build relationships with people across the organization. With people changing roles frequently, the ability to connect through personal relationships became more important as it opened doors into more parts of the organization.

The other decision I made was to take roles that MBAs didn't want. I figured that it would be easier to get a promotion in these areas without having an advanced degree. This strategy enabled me to advance my career more rapidly.

An opportunity to test my management ability came when I was asked to take a role managing the microfilm department located in the bowels of the building two floors below the lobby. This was not a glamorous job and not one I would have sought out when I first started looking for work.

Before the days of computer tracking, paperwork had to be filmed in a sequential way, by day and by work type, so that it could be retrieved when a customer called looking for a correction or copy. There were tens of thousands of pieces a day, each "batched" in a big plastic bag. The bags had to be emptied, papers sorted and everything filmed. There were three employees in the department to accomplish the tasks, one of whom did not have a command of English.

At that time, errors were high and the desire of the employees to fix the errors was low. The place was not only a mess, it was creating many customer service problems. I had seen the customer dissatisfaction first hand while working in customer service. The company wanted our customers very satisfied, so my job was to fix these issues.

The reception I got from the three employees I now had to manage made Linda seem warm and fuzzy. When I said hello and got a blank stare, a grunt and no eye contact from the three people, it occurred to me that I had to find a way to create a connection. I combined communication skills, roles and goals and a sense of humor to break through the barriers. Once they got to know me and realized they were stuck with me until we fixed the problems, they worked diligently to correct the issues.

The changes we made were based on managing by fact and building measures as well as spending time training new working behaviors. In other words, I didn't try to correct employee behavior until we had a way to have a factual discussion about the problem with measured results. By all agreeing we had a problem we could see without assigning blame then tracking progress toward correcting it, we built a team spirit around our progress. Yes, it was a new concept at the time, but it did make it possible for the staff to improve their efficiency; they could see the results of their efforts more clearly. I made sure to give them positive feedback daily on their progress.

In six months we had cleaned up the problem and installed a "quality program" to provide monetary incentives to the employees for low error rates. The employees took more pride in what they did and decreased errors. I had learned that managing was very different than being an individual contributor.

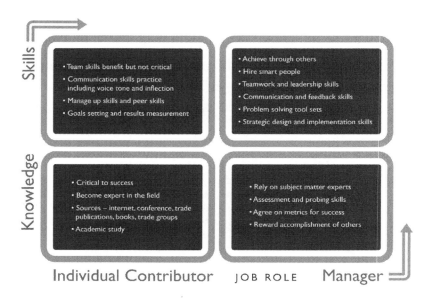

Less than a year after taking the manager role, an opportunity arose to advance a very different set of skills and knowledge. I transferred up to the Legal Department. A forward thinking team up there decided to bring in four non-lawyers to do specific work on segments of the many regulations that govern securities law. The hiring manager was a woman who previously worked in retail sales whom I had met when I cross-trained her in customer service a year earlier. She was extremely bright and had confidence I could do the job. Never underestimate the importance of building peer relationships as they can lead to many positive outcomes in the short and long term—both professionally and personally. You never know when or in what capacity you are going to re-encounter someone who worked above, below or beside you.

This role was a significant challenge and I had considered whether law would be a career worth pursuing when I graduated. I worked as an individual contributor and I had an idea

CHAPTER 5 | Adding New Tools

that I could attend law school at night if I liked the work. The role required immersion in complex regulation and the ability to research and analyze information. We had to review thousands of pages of prospectuses and contracts to ensure they were in compliance with those regulations. I learned that this wasn't playing to my greatest strengths. It also required the ability to write effectively as we constantly wrote regulatory filings and new marketing materials.

When you find yourself being challenged more than you had planned, finding a mentor can be a way to offset your struggles. As I got to know my co-workers and people in other areas that supported the legal work, I found a valuable resource in a man named Tom, who worked in a group down the hall. He helped guide me through some highly complex issues and took the time to share his thought process. Tom was in his late thirties, a Vietnam vet who smoked his pipe all day, filling his office with a haze, at times encouraging one to crawl in—but you should never do that with an Army vet. Tom was a soft-spoken skeptic who challenged everyone to think more broadly, a valuable mentor for me at 25. Mentors are not always people who tell you how well you are doing. In fact they are people who can help you see your areas in need of improvement more clearly. Tom was so skilled that when I needed a person with his skill sets decades later at my new company, I hired him to join my senior team.

One of the benefits of the legal role was that it enabled me to form extensive relationships across the organization and witness the energy of positive achievement at Fidelity that permeated the organization. The legal team was at the center of many decisions across all business functions so there were many opportunities to expand my internal network.

One of these relationships was with Bill who ran retail sales, an inbound call center with 70 sales people. He was one of the most well liked people in the building and very successful in managing his team. When he had a manager spot open up, I asked whether he would consider me for it and made my pitch about why I could do the job. He gave me a chance and in I went as a retail sales manager. It was a risk for him. Up until then, there had been no managers with a background in servicing or legal. We reviewed the roles and goals. Our target was to increase the conversion rate, how many people actually bought our product, on inbound inquiries. Over the coming months, we installed a communication skills process that made our calls more efficient (and less costly) while increasing the effectiveness of each interaction, which led to higher conversions. As the team members became skilled communicators and volumes increased, our assets grew rapidly.

Success Presents Opportunities

Over those first four years working at Fidelity, the company grew substantially on the heels of superior investment performance and became the industry leader. Calls began to come in from "headhunters" and others seeking to lure many employees away to competitors. One day, I got one of those calls. A local competitor wanted to interview me to run part of their retail sales at a minimum of twice my salary, with a significantly higher bonus range.

While I had no intention of leaving Fidelity, I decided to go talk with them. Changing companies brings a very unique set of issues into play. Much like a first date, everyone presents himself or herself well. When I went for my interview, I talked with three people, including the CEO. He made it clear that he wanted to hire me to start this function for them and if I did well I would make a good deal of money and become a vice president of their company. Later that week, I flew to San Francisco for a 10-hour assessment by their retained psychologist to see if I had the competitive nature and personality attributes they desired. Apparently I passed and was offered the job the next week.

I spent a weekend making list after list trying to determine the "right" choice. What I realized is that staying and leaving were both good choices for different reasons. I had to make a decision on what was the right choice for me at the time.

With great trepidation about leaving Fidelity, I accepted the new job thinking the money was ultimately the most important piece. I went into work at Fidelity the next day and resigned.

The last day of work rolled around and I was getting ready to pack my desk with my heart telling me I was making a mistake and my head telling my heart to be quiet and to look at the potential money. At that moment, our senior human resources person, Christine, appeared at my desk. She was professional, street smart, high school-educated, intuitive and always seemed to get what she wanted. She said, "We need to talk."

She explained that one of the most senior people in the organization had a counter-offer for me, but I would have to give her an answer by the end of our meeting. He had decided to make me Fidelity's first "management trainee" and committed to a three-year program during which I would work for a minimum of six months directly for each of his five division presidents. At the end of three years there was not a set position, but I would be placed based on my performance and the needs of the company at the time. Christine reminded me that he ran most of the company except the investment side and I should think about the magnitude of his offer. The pay would be a 15% increase from what I was earning at the time and the ability to get "phantom stock" in the company.

The offer looked like a lot less money than what I had accepted across the street, but it was essentially a working MBA, learning from seasoned, senior people. Choices. My heart and head fought as I listened to Christine's final words, "So Chris, are you staying or packing? You will be working under my direction. This is the only time this offer is being made." Subtle, but effective. I admired her. Counter offers are part of the business world and there are always tradeoffs to be made.

I took the job she offered, feeling it would broaden my skills significantly. I called the competitor back to say that I would not be showing up on Monday morning. Years later, I would hire Christine to work for me as head of HR at a different company, and she was one of my most valued and trusted advisors.

The next three years brought a number of new challenges that would push me far beyond my current skills. Staying positive and open to change were critical components to the resulting success. Change brings opportunity to grow and growth is, by definition, venturing into unknown territory.

My first assignment was working for the properties and purchasing president. His personality was very direct and he made it a point to welcome me to his team and communicate his confidence in the program. On my first day working for him, he sat me down and said, "In the cubicle down the hall we have six years of ledgers (pre spreadsheets, these were financial computer printouts with one entry on each line, tens of thousands of pages of numbers) that cover a number of corporate mergers. I think we have been overcharged by the holding company for interest and want you to see if I'm right." He was sitting with his CFO who was looking at me.

My voice inside screamed, "WHAT? I didn't understand a word of what you just said and it certainly wasn't covered in my history major." What came out of my mouth was, "Sounds good, where's the cubicle?" because I thought that I was expected, as the trainee, to have these skills. The CFO took me down to my cubicle and left.

In front of me were literally dozens of stacks of green binders, each four feet high. I sat down and contemplated what to do. Should I tell them that they might as well have been speaking Mandarin Chinese to me? I had no idea where to even start. Had they overestimated my abilities this much and would I get fired on my first day of the new role? Think, think.

I sat for two hours. I finally called local colleges to see if they had night classes in accounting. One did, starting that week. I signed up on the spot hoping that would give them a reason to keep me. Next I needed to let the President and CFO know that I was going to be slow starting the project, but I would get it done.

I walked down the hall to the President's office and found him with the CFO—and with Christine. Asking if I could interrupt, I said, "Sir, I really have absolutely no idea what you are asking me to do. I have, however signed up for an accounting course and promise I will get the project done though it might take me a bit longer to get started."

All three of them almost doubled over laughing. The President boomed, "We had a bet to see how long it would take you to come back in. We knew you didn't know what to do, but we just wanted to see how you'd admit it. Don't worry, we know you will get it done."

I joined in the laughter, reluctantly. The CFO won the bet apparently. For the rest of the day, he sat with me and helped me lay out an initial work plan that he said should take about ten days to get some basic information. We then had to define "basic information."

I stayed for 15 hours each day that week and completed the work in five days, no doubt to try and prove that I was worthy of the assignment. In the end, after a few months of work, we ended up getting a significant six-figure credit that improved the division's financial position within the company.

However, there was no resting on your laurels at Fidelity. I was immediately assigned a project to solve, of all things, the poor cab service in Boston. Innovation comes from many places and when you happen to be the owner and CEO of a company with billions of dollars in assets like Fidelity and you get a bad cab ride, you can decide you want to start your own car service. Being at the "bottom of the hill" in terms of seniority and having just finished one project, this task flowed down to me.

I was assigned to the savvy purchasing VP and we proceeded to build a business plan that included leasing cars, purchasing a garage and hiring a mechanic and drivers. We completed the plan in four weeks and presented it. In true Fidelity style, the quick answer after presenting our findings was, "Do it." We did and Boston Coach was born. Years later, it would become a large nationwide business with hundreds of cars and thousands of employees. Today, hundreds of companies offer alternatives to local cabs in major cities. One can never underestimate the power of a good idea.

I spent the next month putting the same plan together for a helicopter service between Boston and New York as well as a three-city airline with private aircraft to save business travelers over 90 minutes commuting time. Neither plan was adopted for various reasons, mostly around potential liability and risk. There is a difference between the process of producing results and immediately implementing those results. The skills I learned in terms of purchasing, financial modeling and business planning were all reusable in future endeavors. In fact, many were foundational to my future successes.

I went on to have assignments working for the head of Audit and then working in a new office in Dallas. These assignments were far from exciting, but I continued to build additional skills for the future. As you work through your career, try to stay focused on the long-term potential you have and extract learning from every opportunity you have.

The next phase of my career started with an assignment to help open a new, large, state-of-the-art call center in Salt Lake City. I would be working directly for Christine and be responsible for the hiring and staffing plan for the office, initially over 500 people. We had nine months to complete the site build-out, hiring and operations layout. My role was to design the job specs and a career path for employees, establish salary and benefit levels for all staff and survey the competitive landscape to make sure we could get the needed employees. I would also need to figure out how to hire the phone reps, 400 of them, in one week.

Working with many capable people, we designed a process to do it by taking over a floor of a hotel with many ballrooms and creating a workflow where we could conduct first and second interviews in separate locations, make offers on the spot and then do all applications and paperwork before applicants left. The key was not to alienate the people we didn't hire, as we wanted to have a strong reputation as an employer in town.

We did extensive preparation, with training on interviewing skills as well as role-playing on how to handle the post-interview process. The week arrived and the team began executing the plan. We had a scoreboard in a back room showing the number of people hired and, as it filled towards 400, the team motivation grew and we easily completed the task.

Many of the skills I had learned from previous roles were needed to manage this project—planning, managing by fact, communication skills, critical thinking, peer relationships and others. I was seeing first hand that the time spent building skills was starting to open new avenues for my career. We successfully staffed and opened the office on time and below budget. The sense of team accomplishment we built during that opening process carried over to the culture in the office as the operations started, making it a great place to work for the employees and managers.

The final assignment in my three-year rotation was as a human resources manager of a multi-location division with 2,200 employees who handled all the customer contact for Fidelity. When I had started on the phones seven years earlier, there were 28 of us taking the calls. My history major and graduation seemed so distant.

The rapid growth had fueled Fidelity's employee growth and afforded many people the opportunity for career advancement. As a result, hundreds of the people who had been with

Fidelity since the early days were now part of company management. By promoting internally, the "home-grown" talent had a true sense of common purpose and the company culture was responsive, customer-focused and impressive.

As the rapid growth continued, candidates from outside the company joined and that initial culture began to change as new styles of management were introduced. Later in my career, I would draw on the lessons from this change and strive to build a culture that enabled older and newer employees to stay connected with the culture that made our company successful. It is a challenge to maintain a common sense of purpose and a small-team spirit as an organization grows.

I was offered a permanent role after the program taking operational charge of the Boston call center location housing nearly 700 employees covering sales, service, high net worth and operational segments. The role required coordination with the other three location heads to manage the call volumes.

This was my introduction into a more senior role where the peers were all interested in building their responsibilities, at the expense of others, including me, in some cases. Up until then, I had been focused on building my own skills and managing my own work. The environment added the need to understand other motivations for span of control and power.

The skills needed to be successful in this environment were very different from the ones needed to achieve individual success. I began to shift from being opportunistic to being ambitious and that shaped a new level of learning that would lead to broader responsibility and success. It was also a path that had many more significant challenges, some with negative outcomes.

The skills I used to get to this point would be of value, but not valuable enough to take my career further. If I stayed with the company I would have to add new sets of skills and build different management skills. My eight years at Fidelity had been, in retrospect, some of the best years in my career. In addition to personal growth, I had seen excellent management and leadership models. "Paying your dues" is always a necessary part of growing into future roles and by focusing on the skills you acquired along the way, you will be sure not to waste your time.

When contemplating a change to a new organization, be sure you are going TO a new role not AWAY from your current role. There is a natural tendency to see something different as more attractive than what you have and you need to be objective about the benefits and drawbacks of changing. This is good life advice as well.

Communication Skills

There is a process for structuring conversations to make them more effective and get better results. Many great communicators follow a process instinctively. They find the ways to present their ideas that work best for them and present a compelling case. When you overlay a strong message with a process to communicate effectively, you can improve the power of your message and how effectively you can drive desired results.

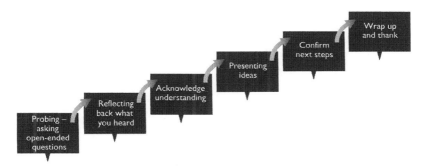

Having a framework for how you manage conversations and interactions is critical to your personal and professional success. Poorly presented ideas, regardless of their merit, rarely get noticed. Conversely, even mediocre ideas presented well can become great successes.

When you perfect the skills outlined here, you will increase your effectiveness and enable yourself to accomplish more work in less time. While these are simple concepts, it is remarkable how few people actually apply these skills to their everyday communication style. Not surprisingly, the effectiveness of using these skills is driven off of the *active listening* skill. Active listening requires that you fully understand the other persons point before presenting your own. Giving visible and verbal feedback showing that you understand is what separates active listening from waiting to speak.

- Segment your conversation into manageable parts. Sometimes you will move through each quickly, other times more slowly, but you will not have to go back over the same information.

- Understand what the issue is you are trying to solve through communication. This means you need to ask questions until the person you are dealing with nods or says something similar to, "Yes, that's it." Use open-ended questions (questions that are not answered by "yes" or "no") whenever you can to stimulate dialogue. Do not try to mix in your thoughts or ideas until AFTER you understand the other person's definition of the issue.

- Before you present your perspective or ideas, reflect back what you have heard to ensure understanding. "So what you are telling me is... Do I have that right?" If you get anything other than a positive response, start again.

- Find a way to acknowledge the ideas or issues. Using phrases like, "That makes sense," "It can certainly help...," "I see what you are saying...," and similar comments that support someone's thinking. This will give you an air of fairness and objectivity. It is not important that you agree, just that you acknowledge.

- Present your perspective. Whenever possible, state where you agree and identify the areas of difference. When you perfect this skill, you can use it to be an effective negotiator by setting the priorities for further discussion. Again, ask for agreement with your assessment and proposed solution. "How does that sound to you?" "Does that make sense?" or similar probes will enable you to assess whether you have enough of a common understanding to move ahead.

- Agree on next steps. These may be to go away and think through ideas or it may be that you have finished the communication and can move on. Either way, state what is to happen next and ask for agreement.

- Close the discussion and thank the person for taking the time to talk through the issue or explain his or her position.

- Through all of this, remember it does not require that you reach agreement every time in one setting. It does require that you act with directness and integrity.

The "graduate work" to be done once you become a master at applying this process is to do so with a measured voice tone, at a comfortable speed and with the use of voice inflection. Your tone and presentation bring across energy level, commitment, excitement and conviction among other qualities. Don't underestimate the effect these traits have on the outcome.

Moving Laterally

Many fields such as medical, legal and science reward increased technical knowledge as a way to advance. Therefore, most people assume that career advancement means becoming technically good at a field and being promoted as you gain more knowledge. There is another way to drive career advancement and that is by building a broad base of knowledge and skills. Focusing your early career, or second career, on acquiring a broad base of knowledge can also produce better long-term results for you. You are positioning yourself to take on more senior management roles later in your career. For instance, if you aspire to manage at a senior level, you will benefit from finance, human resources, sales, legal and many other skills.

Here is the case for moving laterally:

- Pay advances may be faster initially by moving vertically in one segment, but that may limit you years later if there is no more room for upward growth.

- Lateral movement means you may take a new role, many times at similar pay, in order to build your experience base. Building a broader base of knowledge rather than specific expertise can be beneficial later in your career.

- Senior roles in many organizations require a broader base of understanding and skill that are acquired by gaining experience in multiple areas of expertise rather than one.

- Management, by definition, means you succeed through other people's efforts. Those need to be people you trust and in whom you have a belief that they can collectively accomplish a larger task. By building a broad base of knowledge, you are better equipped to manage a diverse set of people towards a common objective or result. You may also have greater credibility with your staff as a result of your experience.

- By understanding the business more broadly, you will be able to make better decisions by applying a broader vision.

- Knowing when to make a lateral move will depend on a variety of factors. If the organization is growing quickly, opportunities can be numerous. In a smaller company, there may be a lack of resources enabling you to increase the scope of your work.

As you look around an organization, think about how you can build more relationships, knowledge, and skills. My story about the finance assignment at Fidelity is a great example of doing something that built more skills for later use.

Managing by Fact

There are two basic ways people manage their teams. *Management by fact* is one and *management by advocacy* is the other.

People who manage by fact tend to address issues more directly and change course based on planned results. Management by advocacy puts a premium on the strength of a person's presentation and the forcefulness of his or her argument. I have seen many leaders who ignore the facts and try to persuade people of the merits of the perspective, only to fail miserably and take many good people "down with the ship."

Management by fact means you will evaluate results based on specific metrics and measures. The old saying that, "You can't manage what you can't measure" is true. Teams can discuss their performance against those facts and seek ways to improve the results based on measurable tasks.

Building a measurement system starts with understanding what "drives" your company's success. Drivers such as customer loyalty/repeat business, ease of access to information and products, accuracy of information, prompt service and sales-per- customer led to successful results in the businesses I managed. Work as a team to define and prioritize these drivers, whatever they may be in your situation.

From these drivers, brainstorm the elements that can be measured and this will show whether you are achieving the objectives set out by these drivers. Then build the measurement systems that will provide regular reporting on your progress.

Management by fact then becomes looking at your results and

designing improvements to change their outcome or increase their effectiveness.

Management by advocacy typically comes into play when the leader of an organization believes in telling people forcefully that they have to do better and then hoping for better results. Here's how you recognize it:

- Does the manager spend time saying things like, "You have to do better" or "We aren't working hard enough"?

- Is there a reluctance to take accountability for bad results?

- Are there amplified voice levels in meetings and presentations?

- Are there budgets and targets put out that are built from unrealistic assumptions?

- Management by advocacy models rely on the loudest or most persuasive voice winning the day. These same people always seem to have a reason why they aren't responsible for negative outcomes.

In my experience, management by fact creates a positive working environment where teams feel invested in a successful outcome. Advocacy works for some people, but they tend to be people who will leave an organization when their message begins to fail.

Peer Relations

Unlike managing up or down, peer relationships are different. These relationships produce the greatest friction in organizations but they are also, many times, the most critical element of success for middle and senior managers.

Here are the challenges:

- Peer relationships have no power differential. You are equals and unless you have shared goals, you can be in constant competition.

- Peers, many times, have different or competing goals. Desired results are not always aligned and therefore decisions are made from different perspectives.

- Peers can be competing for promotions. One person may end up working for the other. People react differently to these opportunities. Competition is a reality, whether overt or covert.

You can make peer relationships work by keeping in mind a few things:

- In order for most peer outcomes to work, there must be a shared success. Be open to solving a problem together and share the credit. Taking all the credit is a quick way to close off future cooperation from your peers.

- Focus on a defined issue when possible. Rather than a battle of perspectives, make it a discussion of a shared problem based on agreed-upon facts and outcomes.

- Peer relations are greatly influenced by personality types. Everyone has preferred ways of interacting; spending time to understand the differences is very helpful. You always want to assess, prior to a discussion, who you are dealing with and what the desired outcomes are for *both* parties.

• Peer relations can be viewed based on the level of mutual agreement and trust you have on various issues. The following chart is a rough guideline.

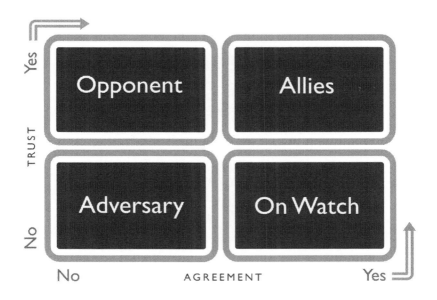

If you trust a person and agree, he or she is an ally.

If you trust someone, but do not agree with his or her position, he or she is an opponent and you will work through the issues together.

If you do not trust someone and do not agree on an issue, he or she is an adversary, meaning they may be more aggressive in their pursuit of their outcome at your expense.

If you do not trust someone and you do agree on an issue, just keep a watchful eye on the process you are involved in together.

Once you understand trust and agreement more clearly, you will know what skills to apply and how aggressive to be in your approach.

Business Writing Skills

Business writing skills are different than the writing classes you took. We now live in an era of "Word of Mouse" where information travels rapidly. While you can certainly build on the mountains of writing feedback you have received over the years, the goals for business writing are different. Business writing takes a number of forms, including emails, memos, presentations and even texts.

- Business writing focuses on outcomes. Be concise and don't embellish.

- State your purpose for writing. Say what you will do, when you will do it and how you will know if a task is complete.

- State what you need to complete the task.

- Summarize the expected results.

- Close with a call to action, *"We need to..."*

- There is never a prize for length. Check yourself for excessive adjectives, adverbs, and lots of "very" types of words.

- State a point once; you don't need to repeat it.

The good news is that you may have acquired strong writing skills in school. Now you want to modify them to be efficient and effective.

Changing Organizations

Any change is uncomfortable, but changing organizations or fields is a reality most of us will face, possibly many times. Change can be your choice, the company's choice or a choice forced upon you due to other circumstances. All of the outcomes require you to step back and evaluate what your options and desires are.

In addition to looking at the new role, there are a few things to think about as you contemplate a change to a new organization:

- Is this organization in a growing field? Is it well positioned within that field?

- Did you ask about its products and services, not just your role? How do they view themselves competitively? How will they stay successful?

- Are they financially sound? If they are on a tight budget you could be let go if the business doesn't meet its targets.

- What is their turnover rate (how many people leave as a percentage of total employees) and why do people leave? You can gain great insights into how happy people are with the company. You can usually ask your interviewer for this information.

- What are the company values? If someone can't answer this or if you ask two people and get vastly different answers, probe further. This inconsistency could be a sign of a weak management team.

- What are examples of potential growth opportunities for you after a few years?

- Have they ever had a layoff?

- What are the benefits the company offers? You want comparable or better benefits if possible.

Decisions – Head versus Heart

Welcome to the great decision-making battle. There will come a time when you have to face a big decision and your head and heart will disagree.

Most of us want to do well in our career. Traits like being conscientious, caring, thoughtful and empathetic are all pieces of our emotional puzzle. But they constantly battle with our rational, pragmatic, realistic and competitive traits.

I've faced many such battles throughout my career. In order to produce a positive outcome, I have found it helpful to identify and accept each component of the decision. Once you complete that process, you can then work to decide what the best path is for you.

Here are a few ideas on how to work through the conflict:

- Get out a piece of paper, a notepad or your computer/tablet.

- Focus on one set of emotions at a time and try to block out the others temporarily.

- Write down all the "head" reasons for making a decision—pragmatic realities that you either must face or believe you need to face. Assign each one a 1-5 rating with 5 being a strong reason.

- Now switch and write down all the "heart" reasons—feelings, loyalties, perceptions that you have. Assign those each a rating as well.

- Re-read a few times and think about what you wrote.

- Remember, the decision is yours, not anyone else's. Put yourself first in thinking it through.

- If you are still struggling, you can visually depict the results using a tool like the one below.

- Are there ways to minimize strong negative elements (making a 3 a 1)? Are there ways to make weak positive elements stronger (making a 1 into a 3)?

Negative Elements Holding You Back

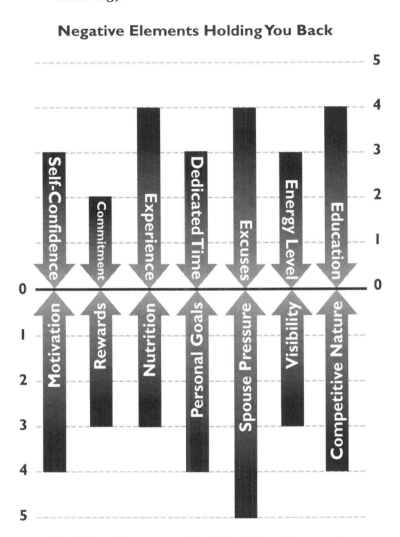

Positive Elements Pushing You Forward

Once you make a decision, then work to make it the right one. Don't second-guess yourself. Put your energy into driving a successful outcome for yourself. It will take work and doesn't just happen, but you need to be committed to your decisions.

You've probably had head vs. heart decisions before. Your parents wanted you to do something but you wanted a different outcome. Your head says to do what your parents want because you live under their roof, but your heart says pursue what makes you happy. This is commonly known as being a teenager. Guess what? This decision process has now changed and you can follow your dreams and pursuits. Good parents will support you in your chosen path provided no criminal activity is involved!

Anyway, you will have more head vs heart decisions. Have the courage to make a decision once you have reviewed the facts. There are almost always risks regardless of your choice.

Business Plans

Plans apply whether you are starting a company, setting direction for an organization, or planning a personal move. The purpose of a plan is to think through the requirements for success in the venture you are about to undertake. By identifying what is important, you can then work to make the outcome successful. The general components of a plan include:

- What are you trying to achieve? What is the purpose of the plan?

- What does the external marketplace look like? How does what you are proposing fit into that existing structure? Are there supporting themes or statistics that frame the solution you are proposing?

- How will you structure the solution you are proposing?

- What resources are needed? People, systems, facilities and support?

- How will you measure success?

- Where will you be located? Centrally, remote or virtually? Will you hire employees, consultants or a combination?

- What are the main risks associated with the idea? How will you address them if they emerge?

- How long will it take to complete the task? How much money is required and how will it be spent?

- Why should the resources be devoted to the idea? What is the projected outcome?

Planning does not guarantee success, but it does increase the chances that you will succeed.

Organization Culture

Organization culture is hard to measure when looking at a job or organization. Basically, you know it when you see it, but that is of little help in an evaluation process. So what drives culture? While many former marketing colleagues will disagree, a company brand is built, not bought. A company can tell me what they are and what they stand for, but if I do not already know based on the product or service they actually provide, telling me is of little value. Those are aspirations—interesting to discuss but not a culture.

Some things to consider as you evaluate the culture of a potential employer:

- Look at the way employees are treated. Is there strong hierarchy? Are the leaders visible and approachable?

- How clearly does everyone you talk with know the company values and vision?

- Is there a team spirit that is palpable? Is it supported and how?

- Ask the HR person why people leave the company. What is the HR assessment of the leadership style?

- Sit outside the office building, without looking like a stalker, and watch people coming in and out. How do they behave? Are groups coming out talking and laughing? Individuals coming out with heads down?

- Talk with friends and see what the reputation of the company is if you can.

CHAPTER 6

Opportunistic to Ambition

My change in mindset was triggered by the imminent birth of my wonderful oldest daughter and then compounded by the arrival of a second wonderful daughter. The "degree of difficulty" in life was about to multiply. When you are living a life where you are responsible only for yourself, decisions are easier to make than when you suddenly realize your decisions will impact little people in diapers. Becoming a parent forces you to realize that life is not all about you and brings focus to the fact that you need to provide for others. A better personal plan is needed.

Building a personal plan means you set goals and work towards them. By definition a future goal requires work to achieve results. One of my goals focused squarely on capitalism—I needed to increase my pay to afford the family expansion and the future education of my children. This epiphany sometimes triggers a need to start evaluating your options, possibly beyond your current employer.

Moving from taking jobs as they become available to planning a career also requires a change in perspective. For many people, their 20s is a decade of great personal growth, much of it marked by going from being reactive to being proactive. It is similar to moving from simply dating to thinking about actually committing to a relationship. You start looking to be more proactive in pursuing your goals.

My years at Fidelity had been professionally isolated and I had done little to build a network of contacts within the industry. One of the changes I made was to be more active in industry trade groups and conferences to build that network. As my career progressed, my goal was to have greater options for advancement in the future by expanding the number of people in the financial services industry that could be part of my network.

So the congruence of knowing I had to provide for a growing family and finding an opportunity for economic growth was about to unfold.

On the busiest day in Fidelity's call center history, a Monday in October, 1987, the company was inundated with over 600,000 calls, three times our normal workload. Panic in the markets had set in. I had arrived at the office before 6 a.m. to review our planned approach with the team and stayed well past 10 p.m. that day and every day that week. As we executed our contingency plans during the course of the day, everyone was under stress, as the financial world appeared to be collapsing. It was the first of a number of financial strains the economy absorbed over the next few decades of my career.

Amid the frenzy, my phone rang and a headhunter asked if I would consider interviewing for a senior role with a competitor. I declined, noting it wasn't a good day to call and I was happily employed. Over the next three weeks, I received three more requests to meet with this company. On the fourth call I agreed. I knew I had to look at what value I had in the marketplace even though I had no desire to change jobs.

After meeting with over 15 senior members of our competitor, Scudder, over the next few weeks, it was apparent that they were going to make me a significant offer with the possibility of becoming a principal of the firm (i.e. ownership stake). My head and my heart began a battle. As I wrote out my lists of pros and cons, talked with my friends and mentors and ran through the possibilities in my head, I began to see clearly that the path you choose and your resulting commitment to success decide much of a career. Once I realized there was not a "right" answer, the decision became easier as it was just a choice and I was lucky to have two good ones. I decided to move to Scudder. Whether it was the best decision or not, I won't ever know. I do know my career worked out well.

On my final day at Fidelity, after eight years and thirteen jobs, I walked to the elevators one last time. The calls kept bustling in, my team members were doing their jobs and life moved ahead on the floor. I was really proud of what we'd accomplished but I couldn't help but be struck by how it all continued on without me. I had invested every effort and idea I had in my work and made contributions to the company's success. Yet, here I was leaving it all behind and taking only the memories, skills and experience I had gained.

The company moved ahead without me and had accepted my choice; I needed to do the same. It made me realize the need to keep a balance between the company and my career. It is important to be ethical and committed and give an organization your absolute best work. But when you leave, you will be leaving your work behind with them. Maintaining a healthy balance by prioritizing your career and your personal plan equally is critical. You are responsible for putting yourself first when it comes to managing your career so make decisions that are right for you, while also being committed to the organization employing you.

As I rode the train home that day, my mind turned to the new role. What lay ahead? Would there be people I enjoyed working with? I assumed that the same level of commitment and drive would exist in Scudder as it had at Fidelity. After all, we were competing for the same customer. I never took time to assess the company culture thoroughly in my job search. As it turned out, I took a step back in terms of working on innovation, but I moved forward in adding valuable new skills to my personal base.

"Welcome to Scudder," the benefits person said at the start of orientation. She went on to explain that Scudder was a partnership and consensus was a critical part of their culture. This was a large shift from Fidelity where you made a decision and moved forward with a plan. A premium had been placed on making decisions in a fast paced world and moving on to the next one. I would soon learn that in any organization the type of management style applied by the top executives drives cultural differences.

After orientation, my new boss led me to my office in a building across the street and said, "Here's your office."

That ended up being the summary of his set of goals for my new job. The situation I was hired for was to start a new department supporting the sales and marketing efforts of the firm. Apparently, there had been a heated internal battle about where my position reported. The Head of Operations had lost that battle to the Head of Marketing. The Head of Operations took the news personally as he was trying to build a larger organization and grab more power in the company. This struggle created internal tension as the two men did not work well together either. Tension among senior executives tends to manifest itself in the interactions of their teams rather than directly.

I had interviewed with the Head of Operations most senior person, Steve, and it had been one of the worst interviews I had ever had. He clearly disliked that the position was not reporting to their team and did not have any hesitation about saying so. He did not look up from his desk and told me he disagreed with the direction and didn't believe the job was needed. Also, he didn't like my background.

My new office was now on his floor, right down the hall. Steve had been instructed to give me fourteen people including two managers. Having just managed 700 people, this size group seemed fairly straightforward. Steve had "reconfigured" his staff the Friday before I arrived and he had given me eleven people and an open position as well as one manager with another open position.

I scanned the resumes of my staff as I unpacked. The manager I was given was an ex-Fidelity person and he had worked in my division at Fidelity. I didn't remember him but I was relieved to find that there was someone who would understand the approach I was going to implement. The rest of the staff appeared to be poor performers according to their reviews, but I decided to make my own judgment after meeting them individually.

It was clear Steve had used the opportunity to shed some of his underperformers, giving the new group the least chances for success. But as it turned out, there were some exceptionally bright people who had simply become disenchanted with their previous roles.

The manager appeared at my door and introduced himself. We said our hellos and I told him I was glad to see Fidelity in his background and asked if he had worked on my team there.

He looked at me and said, "You don't remember me, do you?"

I said, "No."

"You fired me two years ago," he continued.

My immediate response was, "Well, whatever you did don't do it again."

After a couple of awkward seconds, he started laughing. A sense of humor is critical in life and it saved me here. We went on to have a good discussion of expectations and roles. I committed to providing him with plenty of feedback while working to help him be more effective. We didn't revisit his Fidelity days and only looked forward. We built a good working relationship and he had some successes helping to build a new approach to selling mutual funds.

The open manager position needed to be filled. As you should with any open management position, you need to evaluate internal employees and people outside your department and organization. I had spent a number of weeks interviewing employees, one-on-one, to better understand their goals, capabilities and style. I had also observed people around the company as I met my new peers and watched some of their people work.

One individual who worked on our floor for Steve's team was particularly impressive and I had taken time to establish a rapport with him. Don was young and had no management experience, but displayed exceptional skills in connecting and communicating with people. He was considered by Steve's team as not ready for management, primarily because there were others who had been there longer than he had.

I pulled him in to my office one day and told him what I was trying to do with this new group and that there was a need for another manager. He was very interested in pursuing the position. After some pushback from his existing manager, we reached agreement to let him take the position. Hiring people sometimes involves risks, as it is possible to misread someone or apply your own biases, but Don turned out to be even better than I had assessed. He was a highly effective manager, a voracious learner and he became a skilled leader. After a number of years at Scudder, he went on to various senior roles in banking and is now an executive at Amazon.

As the department grew, I hired dozens of managers. As I did, I kept in mind my grandfather's lessons about building groups of people and looked for widely varying backgrounds. In fact, I met a man on the tennis court who would become one of my best managers. Dave was the tennis pro and he was helping me improve my game. He had exceptional interpersonal skills and I could see him being the type of manager that people would gravitate to. Believing that his teaching skills were transferable, I asked him if he had any aspirations beyond tennis. He did, but he didn't believe that he could make a switch after years of doing tennis instruction. He believed he only had the skills to teach tennis; I believed he had the skills to teach virtually anything. I told him I thought he would do well in a business like mine and two months later he traded his racquet in for a keyboard and joined the team.

As you look to build teams, remember that if you manage and lead well, the people who work for you should continue to grow and succeed. Your career success is measured by their advancement and achievement when they are with you and once they have left your team. The actual tasks you accomplish together are rewarding, but seeing personal and professional growth in people who have worked for you is enduring.

The next few years were spent designing a strategy, implementing that strategy, building out a team, creating systems and building budgets to support our efforts and expansion. Scudder grew rapidly from $7 billion in assets to over $30 billion. My organization grew from a dozen cubicles on one floor to a three-location operation on the East and West Coasts with over 680 people.

This was not part of any plan when I was hired; it happened because we achieved success as a company. My role expanded as well and we decided to open twelve storefront locations across the US, requiring me to figure out the best cities, locations, contractors, and service providers and then find staff for the locations.

I also discovered the difficulties of managing remote locations. Managing remote locations is always a challenge and puts a premium on clarity of roles and definition of success. In an effort to maintain continuity between all the new operations, we focused on what drove our customers to do more business with us and oriented our organization on relentless pursuit of those customer drivers. We built on many previous skills such as communication, managing by fact and planning to leverage the work we had done.

During this time I worked on expanding my network of contacts within the industry. I didn't want my career to be limited because I didn't take the time to build relationships with other people who did what I did at other companies. Peer relationships must go beyond your own organization if you desire to have the option to advance your career beyond a single company. Knowing when to stay and when to leave is easier to gauge if you have a broader industry context. You will also know which companies are seeking people with your skills.

When I was in San Francisco for a few months opening our branch there, I had a number of lunches with the head of mutual fund services for a small brokerage firm called Charles Schwab. It was part of the effort to understand a broader range of what was happening in the industry. Interestingly, it also demonstrated that many partnerships in business are built from personal relationships. Let me show you a missed opportunity for significant growth that came from building a network.

At one lunch, we discussed a new idea Schwab had to offer a new way for investors to trade mutual funds. This was 1990, pre-Internet access service. Instead of having a single account at each company, having to call the company and get a check mailed out and then reinvesting it in another fund company, Schwab was going to enable investors to handle the transaction between companies on the same day in one account. It was going to be called Schwab One Source.

They had plans to launch a significant marketing campaign around it featuring a mutual fund family. The whole plan was a brilliant strategy built around a key customer driver, making it easy to do business. They wanted the lead fund company to be Scudder and asked if I could arrange a meeting for them with our senior team. We had first shot at what would prove to be one of the more successful ideas in the business.

With the great performance we had, there was potential for significant new flows of assets to our company without spending a dime. I took the idea back and convened a meeting with the head of marketing and head of product development. They fretted about losing control of our customers and sharing our information about who owns our products with a competitor, but finally agreed to take a meeting with Schwab's senior people.

I arranged the meeting and our CEO decided to join us. At the end of the meeting, Scudder decided not to participate for fear of losing customers. I remember thinking that we were going to lose them anyway because they were going to want what Schwab was building and move there.

On the way out, my Schwab contact said, "We are going to Janus next."

After they left, I relayed that information to our senior team.

Their response was, "Janus is less than half our size and no threat to us."

Six months after the One Source launch, Janus had three times our $30 billion in assets and was growing rapidly. While a networking contact had presented the opportunity to us, a lack of industry perspective had led to a decision to pass on an enormous industry success.

Nevertheless, our division grew beyond anything we projected. We had built a successful, closely-knit management team and their increasing skill levels had propelled our growth and success. We added many talented people with varied backgrounds. We added psychology majors, engineering majors, MBAs and high school graduates. All shared a common trait that they had experienced success in their lives, a key element to someone being successful again.

Not being afraid to hire smart people with varied backgrounds, knowing they will challenge you, is a critical competent of successful managers. Great teams can achieve great outcomes if the leader can let the team perform. I was extremely proud of the team and each member in it.

While my head had kept me pushing hard the last few years at Scudder, my heart was longing for a more challenging role with the leadership style that Fidelity had shown me. My personal plan and ownership stake had kept me at Scudder, as I believed the collective ownership structure would push to monetize the value of the company. It did in 1997 and my role at Scudder ended when we were purchased by a European firm and merged with a competing fund family. I was reorganized out of the firm.

This was a valuable lesson about the business world. Leading any organization requires you to accept that you will be more responsible individually for the results of other people's work. With responsibility comes risk and one risk is that you will lose your job involuntarily. Sometimes there are reasons; other times it is simply a decision based on restructuring.

When I did finally leave, my heart was relieved and my head was happy. It was a very good 10-year period. One of the most important lessons was I now realized that being a leader, rather than simply being in management, was achievable for me. I had worked for 17 different managers in my 17-year career and seen dozens of senior "C level executives" operate with varying levels of effectiveness. I was sure I could be more effective than many of them given the skills I had acquired. The benefit of having exposure to so many different managers was I had seen first hand many effective and ineffective behaviors. Both can be helpful in shaping your style choices when you choose to lead. I felt ready to take what I had learned and, despite not having an advanced degree, lead an organization.

One of the more important lessons from the Scudder time was the role of personality types and how understanding differences is critical to team success. Remember Steve and how we started with a mutual dislike? By each of us gaining a better understanding of what parts of our personality style drove each other crazy, we actually learned to appreciate the skills we each had. Today, 25 years later, Steve is one of my close friends.

Traits that seemed so impossible to overcome when we first met are now seen as strengths. Steve would never give an answer right away and would wait a day or two to respond to a question. In our fast-paced world I had no idea why he delayed everything. Interestingly, his decisions were almost always the correct ones. Steve had a strong introverted side and I was a classic extrovert. We solved problems in different ways and had to learn to leverage those traits. What I didn't realize when I first met Steve in those trying times was that he has some strong fundamental character values and a wonderful family. Had I not been awakened to simple style differences, I would have missed one of my life's strong and consistent friendships.

Personal Plans

Putting yourself first

Previous generations were fortunate to have long careers in one profession, but in today's world organizations often become irrelevant overnight. This reality requires you to base your self-image and self-worth outside your chosen organization. While you should always work hard, be ethical and drive success in the organization you work for, you shouldn't base your self-image or self-worth primarily on that organization. When I left Fidelity I realized that organizations continue on when you go and, while you are valued in the organization, everyone is replaceable.

For that reason, you need to create a personal plan with broad personal goals and targets. Think of yourself as your own company—you want to build a successful organization with a good culture. This personal plan will help you weather the inevitable range of events in your life.

This plan should be directional; it doesn't have to be detailed. I formalized my plan at age 28. My target was to be a vice president by age 30, have an ownership stake in a company by age 35, and meet a financial target by age 40. I added a personal goal of having more than one child by age 36. At age 35, I added a goal of obtaining a senior leadership role by age 45, and the ability to put my kids through schooling without debt by age 50. I have since added a number of new goals such as learning a new field and adding board roles by age 60. This framework, while not prescriptive, helped me focus on making decisions that move me toward my life goals. I was able to weather job losses, economic challenges in the markets and other setbacks along the way because I stayed focused on my personal goals.

Think about what's important to you personally and how you could accomplish that through work. This is different for everyone so be honest and aspirational. Set targets for yourself and believe you can do it. A good life is not one absent challenge, but one built by meeting and overcoming obstacles and being able to celebrate your successes.

Consensus versus Collaboration

The contrast in my job change, going from a decision-oriented culture (Fidelity) to a consensus driven partnership (Scudder), slowed down decision-making considerably. It required rethinking the skills needed for success as well as a re-orientation regarding the process for change and company growth.

Both types of organizations exist and it is important to look at the different ways they operate so you can be most effective in applying your talents.

A collaborative culture that drives decisions typically values:

- Communication and action. Be sure to let people know what you are doing and why, solicit their input; adapt as needed. Then go do the task.

- Having direct communication and feedback in real time so issues don't linger and everyone keeps moving ahead.

- Rewarding results but not at the expense of communication and collaboration. Use of 360 reviews is very common in these cultures to ensure that each person has the tools to effect needed changes and people who aren't collaborative are weeded out. 360 reviews are surveys that are sent to people you work for, who work for you and the peers you work with. Information is compiled and you can clearly see how your style is, and isn't, effective with different groups.

In fast growth organizations, you will touch issues once and move ahead to the next one. Try and make 80% or more of your decisions correctly. The remaining 20% are opportunities to learn what you can do differently the next time.

Consensus organizations value:

- Extensive communication with impacted groups. This usually means lots of meetings. At one job, there were times when we were having meetings to discuss whether we should set up a future meeting.

- Addressing everyone's comments. A decision will not move forward until everyone is satisfied, no matter how remotely he or she is involved in the issue or outcome.

- Delayed decision making until agreement is reached. Instead of acting quickly, these organizations drag their collective feet and move slowly.

- Less emphasis on management by fact because many people are involved who have little knowledge of the business.

- A stronger hierarchy in the organization to ensure that power can be exercised to veto ideas. Depending on who holds the most control, organizations can come to a complete standstill.

This hierarchy leads to greater staff frustration. Staffs need decisions. Decisions are pushed upward and left hanging as uninformed assessment takes place in the upper echelon. At senior levels, too many decisions back up and get superficial review. The lack of understanding means true consensus is never reached and follow through is then diluted because an incomplete decision is made. Typically, this creates more problems, erodes the trust amongst the team and the pattern becomes cyclical. In successful organizations structured like this, good people overcome structural deficiencies.

While consensus organizations can be successful, the growing rapid rate of change will make them less likely to survive. By the time you read this they may be nearly extinct. If you haven't picked up on my personal bias yet, I think they can be challenging to work in for people who value results.

Feedback

Feedback is an important part of learning and measuring how you are doing versus your perception. There are many forms of feedback—verbal, written, peer and subordinate evaluations and countless tools to use. I will focus on verbal feedback here because it is important to be able to give and receive verbal feedback as part of a team.

- When giving verbal feedback it is important to ask for permission and clarify why you are having the conversation.

- Once you have set the stage, describe the situation and behavior.

- Talk objectively about the implications of the behavior and help find alternative ways of approaching the situation in the future.

- You should ask for the recipient's reaction and listen to their views.

- Conclude the discussion with a summary and action plan.

In terms of receiving feedback, it is good to ask for feedback from your immediate boss, peers and subordinates. Seeking feedback saves you from continuing unproductive behavior unknowingly.

- Be genuine about your request and specific in what you are looking for.

- Allow the person you ask time to gather their thoughts and set up a time to talk.

- If you are approached about discussing feedback, be open and not defensive about the request.

- Listen to the feedback and ask questions for clarification as needed.

- If you reach a common solution, summarize the agreement and check for mutual understanding.

- Consider a follow up conversation if needed.

You will always need to deal with constructive criticism and there are ways to prepare yourself.

- Remember that you are at work; no one is criticizing you personally. Just like school, there is always room for improvement so be open and listen.

- Your co-workers are not perfect and are getting feedback too so don't measure yourself against an imagined target.

- Ask for examples and discuss the causes of the feedback.

- Agree to needed changes and then work hard to incorporate them if you agree.

Developing a Contingency Plan

Times of crises are not times to create a plan; they are times to execute a plan. Crises tend to be times when some level of anxiety and stress is introduced into an event. As a result, activities and behaviors that are part of a "normal" operating environment get pushed aside for more reactive and real time decisions. Part of managing a group means spending time identifying the possible scenarios that could derail your business plan.

- What will cause stresses in the business—a competitive event, volume changes, economic or political event, product failure, new business, weather, loss of physical location? While you cannot sufficiently plan for every event, you can cover the events that are most probable to happen.

- Take the time to identify risks and then decide how you will handle them if they appear. What steps will you take and who is responsible for making decisions?

- What will you need in terms of people, support systems, space and supplies?

- Document the needed actions and make sure everyone on your team has a copy that outlines his or her role.

- Repeat the exercise as needed, but no less than annually.

If you do find yourself faced with a crisis, remember this is also an opportunity to accelerate change in an organization. Because the focus moves away from day-to-day routines, changes can be installed more easily as many activities are deviating from standard operating routines already.

Building a Team

There is nothing more critical to your success as a manager and leader than building the right team. Building a team is more than simply hiring the right people, showing them an office and hoping they do well. It requires connection, situational leadership skills, communication skills, feedback and management by fact. There are some fundamentals to start with when building a team:

Hire smart people. Do not be afraid to hire smart, ambitious people even if their knowledge exceeds your own; you have skills to manage them. You are judged now by the effectiveness of your team, not solely by your individual performance. Look for people who know how to succeed first and then assess how they will work within your organization.

You can inherit people as well as get an opportunity to hire. You need to assess people you inherit. Look at previous reviews and work quality. Meet with them and review their role; determine their working style and strengths. My best advice here is to be sure they will perform well for you since your success is judged by their work, coupled with your ability to maintain or increase their effectiveness. If you have your doubts about a certain team member, be sure to set near term deliverables, based on management by fact that will give you information to support or disprove your assumptions. Make changes if you conclude that they are needed.

With people or teams you inherit, do not go in with the assumption that everything was "screwed up" until you arrived. It is natural to want to improve what you now manage, but make sure you value the work that has been done already.

Choose your language carefully, such as, "What you've accomplished here is great. Let's work to find ways you can improve it more; I need your ideas" or "If you could change one aspect of what we do here, what would it be?"

Listen more than you talk for the first few weeks. Make sure you ground yourself in the facts as they are rather than throwing out what has been done and racing to the "This is how it's going to be now" position. Be certain to set expectations with your boss noting that your approach includes evaluation of the current process in addition to planning for change.

Building a team requires clarity. Once you have the people in place and have evaluated what you have to work with, define your expectations, the desired results and the behavior you want. Rather than a lecture, this should be a collaborative discussion in which you guide the team to a result that everyone is committed to. This takes more time than simply telling people but you will have a group commitment to the mission—a critical part of long-term success. It will also set the stage for a team to be more self-managed, with everyone having a stake in the success.

Establish a clear direction and vision. You also need to make it aspirational and have people buy into the vision. How does it improve the organization? How will it benefit customers and employees? What will be the benefits to the team? Challenge the team to define what they can do to support it.

Explain the structure you intend to implement. If you are suggesting changes, make sure you have talked with individual team members prior to announcing them in the team meeting. You need collective, positive commitment to install changes during the meeting. Show why the structure will produce the desired results and how it will function.

Clarify roles and responsibilities of each team member. Have individual conversations prior to a larger meeting to address any concerns. Then you can spend time in the meeting on constructive brainstorming going forward.

Learn as many people's names as you can in your organization. If the organization is small or large, knowing names and taking the time to acknowledge people takes a small amount of time and produces large benefits. In today's world, make an on-line directory with photos and study it regularly.

Support and incentivize the team. Management teams need to have individual and team goals. Setting team performance goals means the team will begin to self-manage and hold each other accountable for results. Having team goals promotes dialogue and feedback, critical components of collective success. In short, you get what you reward so make the incentive systems align with desired results. As a team leader, solicit input, show strong support of the efforts made and publicly recognize achievement. Do not grab credit for yourself; share credit with your team. You will get recognition by their collective performance, not by individual credit.

Focus on developing your team members. Encourage their growth. Provide feedback when you see an area for improvement and be available to them for consultation. As time progresses, learning about them personally (families, interests and activities) builds a stronger bond. As an aside, it has also led to an added gift of many lifelong friendships for me well after we worked as team members.

Realize that you can no longer "do" everything. This concept is critically important to be an effective manager. People have a tendency to come into your workspace when they need something to be solved. Some issues are quick questions; others are complex problems. You must be able to help brainstorm solutions and provide guidance while not accepting responsibility for doing the work, even if you think you could be more effective.

Think of an image where everyone walks into your office with an issue as carrying a puppy. Most of us would love to keep the puppy in the office and watch it grow. But if you take on all issues yourself, you will quickly end up with an office full of puppies and an inability to care for any of them. You will become an ineffective bottleneck. So, your goal with your team is to greet their puppy, feed it if needed and then send them on their way—with their puppy. You will now be able to manage a far greater scope of work and people who work for you will develop greater skills.

If you treat people as subordinates, they will act like subordinates. If you treat them as integral parts of the team's success and value everyone's input, they can accomplish a great deal. Everyone has a perspective. Just because you have the power to command does not mean you need to use it. Save it for times when you need it and, trust me here, there will be those times. When used infrequently, the impact of exercising power is far more meaningful.

Designing Strategy

Whether you are an individual contributor, a manager or a leader, strategy is a critical component to future success. In every role I took, designing strategy had some common elements to produce successful results. There are two main types of strategy, one is designing *innovative strategy* and the other is *operational strategy*.

Innovative strategy is needed where there is a lack of definition around the path you are going to take to achieve an outcome. It requires thinking with complete honesty about the world you are entering competitively.

- What is the competitive landscape and what are the barriers to entry? Can the strategy be replicated quickly? Would someone with superior skills who is taking advantage of digitization be able to make your idea obsolete? Are there regulatory barriers that could disappear and spur increased competition? Can an entity take away your advantage through venture capital backed replication? Is the intellectual property unique?

- What are the economics and does globalization have an impact in cost of delivery? Can you be undercut by low-cost competition? Are your economics sustainable?

- Is the marketplace for your product and service big enough to support many competitors?

- Will customers build loyalty to your brand or switch easily based on price? What is your customer advantage?

All of these questions, and more, need to be considered if you are planning on starting a new venture. The global market-place is highly competitive and ideas can rapidly fail without careful assessment.

Operational strategy is built to take an existing business idea and align the delivery structure in your organization to the strategic goals of the organizations mission. When changes need to be made or the current approach is not effective, a modified operational strategy is needed. To design an operational strategy:

- Evaluate the competitive marketplace. Who has market share? Is there a dominant player? What amount of capital is required? Is there scalability in the product or service? Why is a competitor more successful?

- What are the important drivers of success? Customer experience, low cost, time efficiency, basic needs? Define the ways you will know if the venture is successful.

- What are the economics? What would projected profit margins be at various levels? What is needed for expenses?

A sound operational strategy will maximize the results for the organization. Many organizations spend a significant amount of time building an innovative strategy, but fail to invest enough time in an operational strategy.

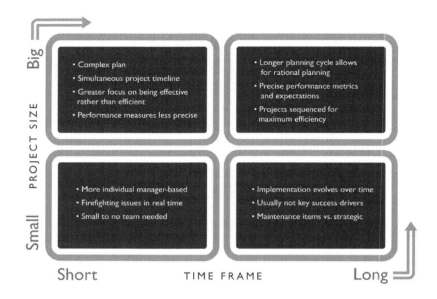

Implementing Strategy

When implementing a strategy, you need a structured process that produces measurable results that can be used to evaluate the effectiveness of your strategic design. When beginning to think about implementing strategy, there are steps to consider:

- Definition of strategy will produce the elements that produce success for the business. These broad objectives, when carried out, will produce a successful business model. An objective is a broad statement. For a sports team, it may be, "Win the Championship." From there, additional steps are taken to formulate how to reach that objective.

- Once those objectives are identified, you need to determine the organizational structure needed to carry them out. Do you need to reorganize? Add staff? Get new equipment? What can you cut out that is no longer needed? Structure must follow strategy to avoid being biased by your perceptions.

- Once structure is formed, operational strategies need to be articulated. These strategies are the specific themes that must be undertaken to achieve the strategic goals. For example, if your objective were to get 100 new customers, your strategy would be to build a sales team having certain characteristics that can achieve that objective.

- Once you have your strategies, you need to build the operating structure within the company structure. Operating structures define each component of the larger organizational structure. What teams are needed, what tools do they need to succeed and how should they be managed?

• Finally, those operating teams need to define their specific tactics for achieving the results. The tactics are the specific tasks that need to be accomplished in order to achieve the strategies.

Now execute the plan and measure the results as the organization starts to function. By building measurement tools based on the specific results of the tactical elements of your strategy, you can make adjustments to your overall strategy as needed. This will save you from pursuing a wrong path, a key area to avoid in today's rapid business climate. You need to be nimble and adapt, regardless of company size.

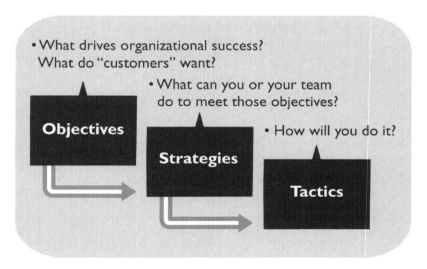

The process of turning strategy into a functioning structure also follows a process and it is a continuous loop.

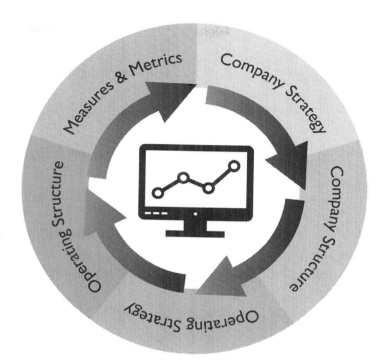

Building Budgets

Building budgets is always one of the more daunting areas, especially if you are a liberal arts grad. It is not as overwhelming as it seems but it does require a methodical process. As I mentioned earlier, I barely made it past Algebra 2 in high school yet I ended up running budgets containing dollars well into the hundreds of millions showing it is possible to overcome early academic shortfalls.

Like many areas, there is a language used here with terms that you do not hear in your daily life. This adds to the overwhelming part. The good news is that a budget is really just an aggregation of detailed data. While certainly not required, signing up for an accounting basics course is a good idea. Knowing the difference between cash basis and accruals and other generally accepted accounting principles is helpful.

Here are some key components to building budgets:

- A "P&L" refers to a Profit and Loss statement. It tracks your actual revenue (profit) and expenses (loss) over a specified period. Think of it as a "real time" finance movie covering a period of time. It is a way of tracking day-to-day performance over time.

- A " Balance Sheet" is a snapshot rather than a movie. It shows the assets and liabilities of an organization on a specific day and values them. Healthy organizations have strong assets (what they own that has a value such as buildings, inventory, equipment). They also have liabilities (mortgages, debts, payments). In most cases, you will see that the assets minus the liabilities equals zero meaning the company is in "balance."

- Most budgets you will build, personally or professionally will be for an annual P&L. The P&L shows how you *run* your organization day to day. The balance sheet is the *result* of financial management of the company measured on a given day.

- Budgeting requires identifying each activity involved in running an organization and assigning it a cost. The accuracy of a budget is dependent upon correctly identifying every piece of cost and income. The results are an outcome of the aggregation of these two categories.

- In building a budget, you will build each "line item." This means you will build a line for each type of revenue or expense; one for salaries, one for benefits, one for supplies and so on. Make a detailed list of each element and give each one a value then sum the total.

- Be ready to justify each expense and show how you arrived at the cost.

- Articulate the risks to the budget. Where can it be incorrect and why? What are the unknowns? What variables could impact it positively and negatively? How will you deliver your revenue or profit?

- You will also need to look at the projected timing of your revenue and expense. This is called building a forecast for your budget. When will monetary impacts be produced and how will they be collected or dispersed?

- Building a budget should be a bottom up process. You identify each item and then start adding them together in groups until every item is accounted for in your budget. Top down budgets are usually inaccurate because they start with saying, "Here's the number we need to hit" and then backing into it through rationalization. If a budget does not produce the desired result, do the strategic work to change it or assess the viability of the business.

- Now you need to manage your tasks to achieve the desired results. If you forget to budget for something, you will need to forgo something else to get the funds or get more funds elsewhere.

Customer Drivers of Success

The best way to achieve results is to define what your "customer" wants and make your organization's goals match them to drive success. In other words, every organization serves a customer. Whether it is a group, a person or an organization, the purpose of your organization will be to make someone feel served. Defining how success is achieved is done through broad statements, not specific tasks. The tasks will come out of the statements. For example:

- What makes customers use your organization more? Easy access, expert information, cost advantage, location? Identify the reasons and make them objectives.

- What are your organizations competencies? Timeliness, expertise, product innovation, services advantages? How do they create success for you?

By focusing on the reasons why your organization or department exists and being very clear on what drives your success, you set yourself up to build capabilities that will drive that success. It will also keep you from undertaking activities that do not tie directly to your success, otherwise known as wasting time.

For example, some of the drivers of success in my mutual fund business were:

- Be easy to do business with.
- Provide prompt, helpful service.
- Provide consistently positive investment performance.

Each of these is broad and we built dozens of tactics beneath each one to ensure our activities aligned to our drivers.

Hiring People

Maximum success is achieved when you hire capable, highly competent people and manage them well. Do not be nervous about hiring people who know more than you do in certain areas. Every member of a team brings capabilities and skills that others do not have and the goal of any great team is to leverage everyone's talents.

- Unlike in school, being smart takes many forms and it isn't defined as being a straight A student nor is it aligned solely to GPA. Skills can be the basis of being smart just as much as having technical knowledge, so believe in what you have.

- Today's world promotes being good at everything during your academic years. To the contrary, I think everyone has areas of expertise and the key is to find them. Then, work on making your strengths stronger.

- Smart people like working with other smart people. When you work to optimize your team's performance, energy will be created and feed on itself. Instead of searching for ideas, you will be inundated with great ideas. Ideas are not the sole territory of leaders.

- Organizational culture is built by how the leaders and managers of the organization act. Their competence and intelligence will permeate the ranks if it is modeled at the top. It is always about showing people what you are, rather than telling them.

- With the speed of change in today's world, you will need as much mental horsepower as you can get to achieve your goals and stay ahead of your competition.

- If you are asked to lead and you do not have people in your organization capable of accomplishing the tasks required, make the needed changes. Your success is directly correlated to your team's ability to carry out their tasks. You need to trust them and believe in their abilities.

Role of a Mentor

A mentor is a person to whom you turn for advice and guidance and who has accepted that role. Finding a mentor, or ideally many mentors, is not just an activity for work. My mentors included my grandfather, a number of teachers, people from work, and a person from a completely different industry. A mentor's role is to be available to you as a sounding board to help you test ideas. Some ideas to consider:

- It is someone you trust and whose opinion you respect.

- It is someone interested in your success and who makes herself available to you.

- It is not someone *who tells you* what to do; instead, it is someone who is there to follow your lead and *help you learn* the skills you need to succeed.

- You need to be proactive in working with your mentor(s). Ask for time and have an idea of what you would like to discuss.

- Do not be shy about building your list of people you can count on. Keep in mind that mentors can become lifelong friends.

- Also, be gracious about giving your time to others as you learn more in your own life.

Personality Types

There has been extensive work done in this field of study in terms of understanding different types of personalities, each with certain tendencies. One of the more common assessment tools is Myers Briggs, developed as a way to characterize personality profiles and then bring about common ways to bridge the differences.

One element to that assessment that I found particularly helpful was the difference between extroverts and introverts:

- Introverts need time to think, process ideas and develop well-thought-out solutions. Being pushed to talk through issues when they are not prepared drives them crazy.

- Extroverts prefer to talk about issues in real time and work on a solution together. "Why wait? Let's just deal with it now," is their attitude. Needing time to go away and think is seen as an avoidance technique and drives them crazy.

- When a strong extrovert meets a strong introvert without any knowledge of this difference, there is a high likelihood of a poor relationship, even genuine dislike.

This describes Steve's and my initial relationship at Scudder. We did not know why we didn't get along at all until we attended a session that gave us this information. Instead of continuing to miscommunicate, we understood it was our innate styles that had caused the previous dysfunction.

Once the issue was identified, we were able to fix the problems. I learned to truly value an introvert's thoughtful approach and realized the level of thought and preparation when discussing a solution was complete. This approach is an invaluable part of a team when known and leveraged.

When you get "stuck" in a working relationship (or at home for that matter) take time to understand personality styles and you may learn a great deal. Different approaches are what improve results when you take the time to learn what each has to offer and how it can be leveraged within a team structure.

CHAPTER 7

Learning to Lead

My opportunity to lead was about to present itself. Even though my Scudder days ended differently than I had expected, I was well positioned for making a positive career move forward.

After leaving Scudder, I made contact with many of my expanded network of colleagues, ex-Fidelity, industry, competitor and friends. One of them, a Fidelity peer, had taken a senior position at a company that owned 14 different asset managers including some well-known brands. He and I met to touch base so I could solicit his ideas about job opportunities. As our discussion progressed, he indicated that he wanted to get a company started within their portfolio that would aggregate common services in the companies they owned, resulting in lower costs. The challenge was that no one was going to force the companies to move their business so it might not be possible. I decided to take a chance and I told him I would do it. If it didn't produce savings in two years he could send me on my way. It was a career risk but it was also a way to get a shot at a leadership role in a company. He spoke with his boss and they agreed to let me do it, using one of their companies as the "seed" business. From 1997 to 1999, we built a team, systems and capabilities that would enable our peer companies to save significant costs for their companies and shareholders.

As it turned out, the 2000 market crash proved to be a catalyst for the companies to try to cut expenses, which played right into the business plan we had established. Our company benefitted from the cuts in the affiliate companies and consequently the overall holding company benefitted. While these types of events can't be planned, our having assembled the business plan, internal capability and team to run the company gave us the opportunity to assist in a difficult time. Careers do have an element of luck and timing that cannot be predicted, but preparation and sound business planning enable you to take advantage of those times when they happen.

Senior Team

I had the leadership job I had been seeking as a President/ CEO. The challenge then became to build a high-performing team that was highly competent in their roles. Because I knew that my role was to drive group performance and not to do their work for them, building trust was a key component. In order to build trust you must have the ability to self-regulate your behavior and approach as a leader. The words you use and decisions you make come under greater scrutiny from those who work in the company. As team members try to position themselves for success, they will take their cues from your actions. Your role is to ensure that the team functions at a high level, the business is financially sound and that you are spending time growing the business and communicating the vision.

The seed business came with a staff and I began my assessment process of current capabilities and needed team additions or replacements.

Looking inside the organization first, there was a very bright legal counsel who ended up being a co-founder and key architect of our operating model. He had a keen mind that worked faster than just about anyone I had ever met. Because his mind worked so fast, most people around him were left behind quickly and some didn't particularly care for his style. He talked over them at times rather than listening to them. I believed that could be fixed by working with him on active listening skills. In fact, we worked on them together for a couple of years and he saw great improvement in his leadership. Removing that impediment to his style enabled our company to benefit more fully from his strong business and legal skills.

We needed a strong human resources person to help grow the company, skilled in all phases of the job. We needed a strong extrovert here. I knew the perfect person was someone I already knew—Christine. I have already highlighted her numerous skills. She joined the team and became a confidant for everyone on the team (and seemingly in the company). While I know she handled many issues that I never heard about, she was invaluable in providing direct feedback about my effectiveness in various situations, keeping many small issues from becoming larger ones. To be an effective CEO, you must have someone who knows you well, knows your people and has their trust. Christine has always been a model of an effective human resources executive—intuitive, direct, a skilled communicator, having a sense of humor and pleasantly relentless. She had been an early mentor for me and I still turned to her when I wrestled with various decisions in this role.

One of our key risk areas was a group called Fund Administration. If the job was not executed perfectly, every day, there was significant financial risk that could damage the company and its ongoing viability. I needed a strong leader who also had impeccable planning and execution skills. The person running it was retiring and his "number two" person did not have the leadership characteristics to take his role. I ended up, after 18 years, calling Tom from my Fidelity days.

He was blunt and I could always count on him to challenge ideas without fear of disagreement. In addition, when interviewing him I asked if he could tell me an example of a time he had made an error and how he corrected it.

He thought for a minute and said, "I don't believe I have made one at work."

Normally, that would be a red flag for someone in denial but knowing Tom and his integrity, I knew he was stating a fact as he knew it. As a Vietnam vet, Tom told me later he kept a list of "the five people he would be in a foxhole with" meaning he trusted working with them. If you weren't on the list, there was an element of impatience about having to deal with you. Interestingly, Tom was one of the best mentors I have ever worked with and left a long line of bright, capable people scattered about the industry. I was thrilled years later when he retired to hear that I had cracked the top five (even if only briefly). Throughout our years working together, I always checked my thinking with Tom, even when I knew it would come with a lecture about my leadership deficiencies.

A strong CFO is someone everyone dislikes equally because he or she has to say no to spending requests regularly. It is similar to asking a parent if you can borrow the car when you were younger; you didn't want to hear, "No." If you can find an individual who people actually personally like, you've made it easier to function well together. We did. I was conscious that the parent company CFO was skeptical of the idea behind our company and would, because of his style, be highly critical of every request we made for funding. So I hired one of his people, Scott, whom my ex-Fidelity colleague recommended. He helped buffer the interface to the parent company. He was young, so inflexible he almost snapped just sitting in his chair and was not one to engage in philosophical discussions. Perfect I thought. He just needed some coaching on retaining his effectiveness while becoming part of a team. As he has matured in his career, and worked on the feedback he got, he became an extremely effective CFO while also becoming a key part of our management team. He would proactively look for ways to move the business forward and partner with the other team members to find solutions. While his flexibility will always be appropriately rigid, he learned to be a good partner on the team. I did get a laugh when I saw him at the gym and he refused to stretch. Some traits are ingrained and cross over the work/personal habits line.

We would be delivering systems-capabilities to affiliates and needed a strong leader who understood both system operations and applications. We needed to run "the plumbing" but also build the applications to grow the business and increase efficiency. This is a job, when done right, that is virtually invisible. When done wrong it can sink a company. It was a role designed for a strong introvert. From a competitor, we had hired an exceptionally skilled woman, Diane, who was highly adept in all facets of technology. She was mature, introverted and didn't engage in conflict without some sound reasoning. She deferred to louder voices, of which we had plenty on the team. Working to have her voice carry more weight was the challenge I consciously undertook in meetings and tasks. She was, in most cases, the steadiest voice in turbulent times.

Finally, the lead operations role needed to be filled. There was a potential internal candidate but she chose to move with another part of the parent company. I called Frank after 15 years of not seeing him. He had been working at various competitors and was ideally suited for the role. He accepted and I added a third former mentor to my team. Frank still had his compassionate, effective working style that drew people to him. He would have the largest team within the company and having complete trust in his abilities was a critical hiring factor.

I had a team of high performers, all more senior in their roles than we needed initially and only three of whom had worked together before. We needed to build a high-performing team out of the group and grow the company. With this type of team, facilitation skills are required to achieve high performance. We had to tackle some complex issues that required everyone's input:

- Design scalable service offerings that could be used by large and small companies.

- Negotiate and secure group-buying power for services before actually having business from any customers.

- Build lower cost, higher quality operating models than current practices in the portfolio companies.

- Sell the ideas into management teams that didn't even know they were looking for a solution, yet.

These issues would all require a cohesive management effort and a strong focus on success factors. They required becoming very skilled at situational leadership. I needed to blend strong personalities that had competing, and equally valid, viewpoints. I found that doing it effectively required everyone's efforts, not just mine. Our success was achieved because we all took responsibility for making it work rather than building a "command" structure where everyone waited to follow orders. This type of high-performing team gives everyone a stake in the outcome and functions in a way that rarely requires an authoritarian decision. Where a command decision was required, I made it and we moved ahead.

We used a variety of tools to craft our initial and ongoing strategy; stakeholder analysis, SWOT analysis, force field charts, prioritization tools and ranking systems. The business grew from no revenue to over $35 million a year in 5 years and our financial contribution to the holding company was exceeding the plan. As our holding company became more successful, we became a more attractive target for buyout. The holding company sold itself to a French bank conglomerate and we all began the process of integrating new business and financial requirements.

After seven successful and enjoyable years with that team, I was recruited away. Bank of America had just purchased Fleet Bank and the heads of both of the mutual fund businesses left during an industry event known as the Market Timing Scandal. I was asked to join their mutual fund business as President and CEO of the Columbia Funds and perform a large consolidation of both banks products and operations.

This would be the greatest challenge of both my skills and acquired knowledge. Greater skill levels would be required to navigate a significantly different business structure.

Before looking at that challenge, take a minute to think about leaders you have had in your own life. Leaders do not have to be "famous" or well known. Yes, there are presidents, sports figures and social leaders. There are also great teachers, captains of your teams growing up or social leaders. My guess is that each one brings to mind a different set of skills and different approach or style. While leadership implies being at the top of a group, the ways to lead are varied and what is effective for one leader is not for another. The ability to be self-aware and know what you can do well is what makes you an effective leader.

Leadership requires different skills than managing. While there are many managers who are put in leadership positions, successful leaders apply skills beyond those needed for management success. Here are some examples:

- Articulating a vision and energetically engaging all parties involved. In most cases, the vision has to extend beyond what people think is possible and challenge an organization to achieve beyond its current level. The vision needs to be concise and delivered with a context that frames it in the reality of the world it serves. Every person in the organization should be able to align his or her work with some part of the vision's objectives.

- Creating simplicity is critical. A leader must be able to communicate clear objectives and, regardless of how complex a situation is, the leader needs to make it tangible for people.

- Inspiring commitment and loyalty to the cause. Traits such as personal integrity, trust, confidence and ability to engage others are all valued here.

- Creating an atmosphere that motivates people to achieve their best.

- Valuing everyone involved and constantly making a connection that shows people they are valued.

- Sharing recognition and rewards, knowing that your success can only be achieved through the efforts of others.

- Accepting all questions, comments and critiques and offering perspectives, facts and wisdom in answering them.

- Promoting transparency and open dialogue amongst colleagues.

- Measuring success and communicating progress, good or bad.

- Adapting to changing circumstances and handling them with reason.

All of these qualities weave together in strong leaders. Leaders must create a path where there isn't one currently. They are expected to provide light when others see dark and are criticized when their plans do not produce the desired result. But leaders know that they must be acting and taking the risks of criticism in order to achieve success.

As I entered my 18th year in the business world, I would get a chance to shape my own leadership style and risk the possibility of failure in order to become a leader. When leaders lead, there will be people who agree and people who don't. Leadership is about accepting a challenge, knowing that you have responsibility for the outcome while understanding that success will be achieved through the efforts of many people, not just yourself. Great leaders make this feat look effortless while others appear to be in a constant state of crisis.

I have always viewed leadership as a set of styles, not one hard-driving style. Developing an appreciation that leadership takes so many forms is possible when you try to view it from different perspectives.

One visual analogy I like to use to describe leadership is to think of climbing a mountain. Chances are there are multiple routes to the top and many choices to be made along the way. If a leader simply starts charging up the hill and yells to everyone behind her, "Come on, let's go" the leader will miss that some people may get injured, they may not be able to climb, or they may drop out. At the top, the leader will commend those who made it and admonish those who don't. Other leaders may climb with the group, sometimes leading and sometimes following. They will participate in decision-making and communication, taking care to ensure that everyone reaches the top. Finally, a third type of leader may realize they have superior climbers and turn them loose while following them up another route.

In all three cases, the leader has accomplished the goal, but think through how it would feel to be part of each team. Would you prefer to climb with one versus the other? Each one had varying levels of success just as each leadership style could be characterized as successful. As you develop your leadership skills, you will have to decide what type of leader you want to be and act accordingly. There is not just one style of leading and different personalities get desired results using different styles.

Self-Regulating

As you gain more responsibility, you also receive less direction and, many times, less feedback. You need to be more proactive in driving results. If you cannot look at your work objectively, you can develop a false sense of reality and habits that are not productive. Since you are often told by people around you when you are a CEO that everything is great, whether it is or not, a critical component of becoming an effective senior manager is the ability to regulate yourself.

- Evaluate yourself as you would someone working for you. What are you doing well? What needs improvement? Are there any issues needing immediate attention?

- Set realistic targets. Making 100% of decisions correctly is not a realistic goal. If you assume you should get 80% of them right, by definition you will get 20% of them wrong. Try and learn from those 20% and be candid about your role in them.

- Be thoughtful in your choice of words and pay attention to how you present your ideas. Are you being forceful, inclusive, dismissive or directive in your tone? Pay attention to both your verbal and non-verbal habits. Take time to think about what you want prior to presenting your ideas where feasible.

- Ask people for feedback. You need to have people who will be honest with you in your life, but even those people will need to be asked for feedback. Make offering this feedback safe and encourage honesty. Even if you disagree, listen and thank them.

Creating High-Performing Teams

High-performing teams require that you hire high-performing people. Many times, groups of very capable people have clashes in personal style because they have not all reached their level of success using the same skills and approach. So meshing a team together is a process that a leader must undertake, knowing that it will take time and not happen just because he or she declares it will.

The team I outlined above was a team of individual stars in their disciplines, but we faced some challenges in blending their talents together. The process we used to be effective in accomplishing this blend follows a framework that is a skill to be learned: *Storming, Forming, Norming and Performing.*

Storming is challenging because a common team framework must be established and some parameters about behavior must be installed. Like any group, everyone has to find his or her place in the team. It is a period that can have times of conflict and disagreement that must be resolved. A good leader works with the team to ensure each person understands that all roles are important and that common definition of those roles is understood. In this phase, objectives and metrics of success are developed and agreed upon. You can't manage what you can't measure. You will need many of the skills outlined previously to be effective here and there will be times where you question the ability to achieve a successful outcome. Definition of shared work as well as individual work must be agreed upon. In my experience, taking a team off-site and spending a concentrated, well-facilitated day or two working on team dynamics is a great investment. We used filming of the team as a tool to illustrate how people's behavior impacted others. It's humbling and amusing with the right team.

Forming is a stage that evolves when team members finish the work of understanding roles and measures. The team leader will have effectively established the team operating structure. The team begins to form its working style and the leaders role becomes one of fine tuning interactions and facilitating, rather than installing wholesale change.

Norming is the process of creating efficiency and effectiveness in daily work. Normalization means a team has become consciously competent of their collective goals and understands what they need to do to deliver their share of the resulting success. Again, aligning incentives with the expected results here will increase the speed of adoption.

Performing is when a team has mastered their working behavior and operates as designed as a standard practice. Since they have completed the base work to be effective, they can now strive for peak performance and optimize their ability to create collective success.

High-performing teams do not just happen. They are the result of a planned process that builds on the ability of each member to contribute. It makes them feel motivated to contribute their best efforts for the collective success of the group. Leadership sets the tone and creates the environment for this change to take place.

Situational Leadership

I have often been asked, "What is the most important skill to possess as a leader?" In my opinion, situational leadership is it. It is a skill that requires the leader to adapt his or her style to each situation, not each person.

Not everyone who works for you is good at everything. There may be a lawyer who negotiates contracts with ease, but if asked to design a systems application would be lost. While individuals can be high performers in their job, they need different management direction depending upon *the tasks* they are being asked to do. It is up to the leader to recognize what skills are required for each task.

Attached you will find a 2x2 depiction of the options a leader has when thinking about how to provide direction to each situation. Leaders who become unconsciously competent at this skill and apply it in all their management dealings, are by far the most successful leaders. My experience was that this skill built great communication and strong loyalties because it demonstrates that you, as a leader, are thinking about how to make the person you are dealing with successful.

There are four styles of leadership:

- *Directing.* When you face a situation in which the person you are assigning to a task has little or no experience to draw from, you need to be directive. "Here are the steps we need to do" or "Start by doing this." The person can then start to do specific, defined tasks without having to come up with what they are.

- *Coaching.* If a person has some skill, but not a high level of confidence or competence in the required task, you need to apply coaching skills; you become the teacher. "Yes, that would be a good next step; how would you design that?'" What would this task require for resources?" Questions like these are at the heart of coaching. You want to ask open-ended questions (those that cannot be answered by yes or no) that help the person think through the task at hand. Even though you may already know the answers, people learn more when they solve the problem than when they are told the answer. Time invested in helping people develop their critical thinking skills pays off eventually because they "self coach" themselves before even coming to you next time.

- *Participating.* Leadership here shifts and you become more of a peer in the process rather than a director. Remember, leadership is not always standing at the front of the line and yelling, "Come on, let's go!" Sometimes it is standing next to people and steering together, and sometimes it is being in back of the group and herding any stray thoughts. Participating is standing with people and being part of the decision making process. Others may define needed tasks and your role is to ensure all tasks are done and no missteps take place. The person being managed develops his or her own momentum and you act as a resource. Typically people are fairly competent at the required skill initially and may need less guidance to complete the tasks.

- *Delegating.* When you have a person who is highly competent at a task, he or she needs little direction and oversight to complete the task.

Intervening could even slow the completion down. When delegating, the need is to agree on the desired outcome and timeframe, then observe. An important lesson here is that there are many ways to complete tasks. Whether completion is done exactly the way you would do it or in another way is usually irrelevant. Let people use their style. You can give feedback, if needed, on effectiveness when the results are in. Regular "check ins" are helpful. Pop your head into the office and say, "Everything going okay on X project?" You can usually get enough information to ensure the task will be completed.

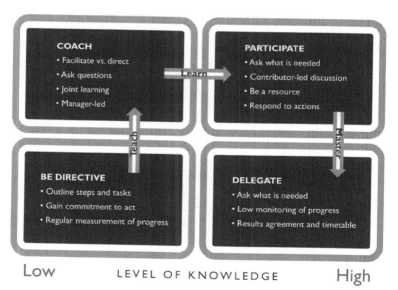

Facilitation Skills & Running a Meeting

Leading any high-performing team, whether or not they report to you, requires facilitation skills. The reason most groups have meetings is to solve common problems or brainstorm issues. By definition, that would mean there will be different perspectives in the room. When you overlay that with different personality styles, the need for strong facilitation skills is paramount. The ability to move a process forward and resolve any issue impeding progress is directly related to the effectiveness of facilitation.

Strong facilitation looks effortless. Think of it as directing airline traffic and there are no accidents. Must be easy, right? No, it is a direct result of the skill of the person facilitating.

There are primary facilitators who lead the discussion. Other people in the meeting need to be secondary facilitators meaning they should take an active role in resolving issues instead of waiting for the primary person to identify all the issues.

Here are a few ideas that can help make meetings more effective:

- Have an agenda. Know what you are trying to achieve.

- Be flexible. Just because meetings are booked for a period of time doesn't mean they shouldn't end if the objective is completed early.

- Facilitation does not mean telling everyone the answer. Use techniques that enable the best ideas to come forward. This requires the facilitator to be a neutral party and ask the appropriate questions to gather the information then lead the team to a decision. As teams mature, a facilitator can take more latitude in stating an opinion but this requires teams to reach a "performing" stage of development.

- Moderate the interactions of team members to ensure that all voices are heard. Teams tend to defer to the loudest voices or strongest personalities. Good facilitation ensures that all ideas are given equal merit and all people get to provide input. Execution of a plan will require all participants to perform and all need to be bought into the approach. The only way to ensure that this happens is to drive involvement actively, not passively. When running a meeting, be sure to ask everyone for input directly.

- Be conscious of airtime, yours and others. Make sure no one person dominates the conversation.

- Keep the conversation on track. Defer issues that are discussions for another time. We had a practice of having a sheet labeled "Parking Lot" on the wall where we would park an important but off-point topic. It would get dealt with another time.

- Keep the meeting focused on the purpose for meeting and document results. Review results, timeframes and people accountable for completion before leaving the room.

- Do not schedule meetings to plan meetings.

The basic components of leading a team are situational leadership and facilitation skills with use of effective process tools. Process tools are methods that are used to drive decision-making. Like all the skills in this book, you will have to work to learn them and incorporate them into your own style. Once you do, regardless of whether your title is CEO or supervisor, you will become a more effective leader and you will enjoy the benefits of working with exceptional people.

CHAPTER 8

Influence Without Power

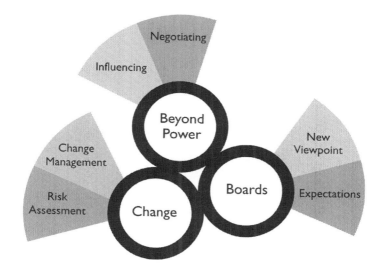

G oing to Bank of America created new challenges that were unique to an organization of this size. Few companies in the world are as large and my entire career had been spent in companies a fraction of the size of this one.

The company had 300,000 employees and an organizational structure that created a matrix of support (technology, finance, human resources, etc.) all reporting into different parts of the organization. Columbia Management, the bank's asset management business, generated well over $1 billion in revenue, but that number was dwarfed by the more than $100 billion in revenue generated by the entire organization. Columbia Funds made up over 80% of Columbia Management.

Instead of having people reporting directly to me who managed all aspects of the business, we had to rely on "business partners" whose activities included a far broader scope than just our business. The bank chose to have functions that were common to many business segments operate independently from the areas they served.

The direct control of the process and outcome that had been so common in other organizations was replaced by the need to persuade others who, at times, had unaligned goals. There was a strong emphasis on a specific leadership style rather than leveraging diverse leadership talents.

Even though the title said president, my ability to drive performance was dependent on gaining the support and performance of groups that were integral to our success, yet I could not drive their priorities. The skills needed to operate and be successful were based on influence and negotiation rather than developing, managing and executing a plan.

Dedicating resources took much more administration and paperwork than in smaller, more nimble structures. There were many times when the need for overall company performance took precedent over the priorities of any individual business unit. This created an underlying tension between colleagues.

These factors created a very different set of challenges than any I had faced in my career. However, I was excited by the challenge and interested to see how the skills I had acquired would work in such a different operating structure.

The primary reason I was hired was to take a large number of smaller fund groups that the bank had acquired and turn them into one $350+ billion single brand, Columbia. This role would require the most significant "change management" challenge of my career.

Fund companies have some unique characteristics. Each is governed by an independent board, creating a check and balance system with management that provides protection to the underlying shareholders. As fund president, my obligation was as a fiduciary (a person representing the interests of the investors) first and as a bank employee second. Priorities did not always align and hard choices had to be made. I also needed to balance the board's role with the banks desire. When fiduciary duty collides with capitalism great delicacy is needed to persuade all sides to choose the right path. These were the most difficult skills to use as the outcome was based on the power of a persuasive argument. Having facts identified and at my command was critical to establishing the credibility needed to drive the decisions.

One of the biggest challenges came in merging the independent boards that had been overseeing the individual fund groups as we consolidated the funds. Most fund companies have a single board. In order to merge, some boards would have to vote themselves out of a job. As you can imagine, this is not a vote that most boards do intuitively. While we had no direct power to make them do so, we were successful in reducing the number of boards by more than half using fact-based management.

The boards were only one of over two dozen stakeholders (or entities) that had an interest or oversight of some portion of the consolidation. There were federal regulatory bodies such as the SEC, state Attorneys General, independent compliance officers, internal bank risk officers, finance departments, auditors, legal teams, compliance teams and many more groups that had an interest or "stake" in the outcome. Each had their own agenda and few aligned. This situation created a complexity that went far beyond simply executing projects and making changes. The dynamics of every different stakeholder having a different agenda and wanting different outcomes could have caused institutional paralysis if lead incorrectly. It was also guaranteed that each step would have at least one critic.

Any time directives were used rather than influence, I had to accept that there would be strong critics.

When faced with so many competing interests, leaders need to articulate a clear vision and plan, knowing there will not be complete agreement. We could then move forward and communicate our progress towards completing the plan while also trying to address each of the stakeholders issues as we proceeded.

To compound the challenge, we were given nine months to complete a process that our plan indicated would take two years. In fact, the target timeframe was so extreme that one member of the existing senior team resigned saying it could not be done and he did not want his career tainted by the imminent disaster. He resigned only after making his viewpoint known to the rest of the team. These are situations that require you to react and how you handle them will send clear messages to your group. I chose to acknowledge his concern and then present how we would execute the plan in specific detail rather than debate him. By increasing everyone's knowledge of the entire plan, rather than just their own piece, we built a focus with the remaining team that led to them being more supportive of each other. I never addressed the implied lack of confidence in leadership he expressed directly; I did it through fact-based management and clear articulation of plans.

The sheer number of projects, over 10,000, that had to be completed simultaneously was staggering. Due to the artificially imposed deadline, these projects would have to take place side by side rather than sequentially, as they would have if a logical work plan had driven the process thus increasing the risk of failure. If one project timeline slipped meaningfully, it could have a cascading effect on others.

This level of career risk creates a whole new level of thought. I had accepted the change in cultures as I had probed during my interviews for company habits. I accepted that there was a risk of failure, but was equally aware of what it would take to complete the project. The major unknowns going in were the personalities and styles of the leaders I would be working for and I underestimated the amount of administration required for every decision. The lesson here was that no matter how well you plan, variables will always arise that cannot be planned for, whether they are people, politics, markets or are socially related. All the skills I was armed with enabled me to adapt to these variables.

I certainly understood that this challenge would call on all of my skills starting with attitude and effort. I had to convey confidence and positive energy to the organization. All of the past skills around planning, roles and responsibilities, strategic implementation and others came into play during these years.

New skills were also required. Risk assessment became important in all facets of the business, not just investing. Enhanced skills were needed in influence, negotiation and stakeholder analysis.

Fortunately, there were a number of very skilled people on the team who rose to the challenge and we all had the satisfaction of completing the task in nine months. We immediately turned our attention to driving the success of the resulting organization. We found that moving nimbly was not possible in a matrix organization and our ability to react to a rapidly changing marketplace was slower than many of our competitors. After five years, multiple acquisitions and a financial crisis in 2008, the bank decided to sell Columbia to Ameriprise. I would not be going with the company.

The mutual fund industry had changed during my 30-year career from a high growth business to a mature marketplace. Measuring market share and avoiding risks replaced being innovative through taking risks. The financial crisis in 2008 devastated many investors. Their investing behavior, mainly their level of trust changed significantly. The job content changed from being energetically creative to measured maintenance and execution, a common progression of a maturing industry. The industry began consolidating with deals like Merrill Lynch being purchased by Bank of America.

While there was certainly a role in the industry to lead another organization and maintain the business, I didn't find that compelling. I enjoyed start-ups and turnarounds because they required an energy that doesn't exist in maintenance roles. I wanted to find complex challenges and ways to contribute to a different industry.

I began to contemplate how to shape the next 15 years of my career. Going back to many of the skills outlined earlier, I concluded that a new challenge in a new field, while still using all the skills I had learned, was my new direction. I also had a desire for greater flexibility in my life to be able to pursue non-work interests. I decided to pursue board roles as a way to stay involved in senior level decision-making while also doing some consulting and executive coaching.

Board roles are different than management roles (non-profit boards are an entirely different discussion). When you lead a company or organization, you have to be involved in the design and execution of the business plans in addition to managing the resulting risks. While there are different types of boards, from founding boards to governance boards, in general the rule for board members is, "Nose in, fingers out." This means the job is to assess management's plans from the viewpoint of an objective observer or fiduciary and ensure that the risks are being identified and addressed.

The purpose is to balance the management perspective with sound business principles and avoid practices that would result in financial, regulatory or compliance trouble, among other pitfalls. Many management leaders have trouble making the transition from management to governance, as they do not have skills to change their approach. Effective board members can take their experience and provide management the benefit of it through open-ended questioning, challenging and acting as a resource to the senior team. Ideally, boards pay attention to the composition of the board and add members with specific, non-redundant skills.

My experience was put to work on a board in the electrical power industry, once again reinforcing that the skills you just read about are transferable. I entered another field where I had little knowledge of the business, but everything I had worked on for 30 years could be applied. My goal is now to build a board portfolio and bring value to a variety of business endeavors through consulting.

Change Management

Implementing significant change in any organization requires strong leadership. If there are time constraints, it may be necessary to "tell" people what to do versus "sell" them on the merits of the change. In those cases, getting people to truly buy into the change is somewhat compromised, but can be successful if the leader has credibility with the group. In implementing change, a structured process needs to be installed.

Consider the following when managing change:

- Articulate a vision for the change. What is the desired outcome and why is it needed? What will the end structure look like? What are the objectives, strategies and tactics?

- Document and analyze the current structure or process. How does it work today and what are all the components?

- Identify the needed changes, or gaps, between the current structure and the desired outcome.

- Document all projects needed to fully effect the change.

- Identify the time, resources, cost and responsibilities to each project

- Create an overall timeline sequencing the projects from start to finish. Determine the capacity of people needed to accomplish each task.

- Aggregate the projects and the needs then start to communicate with all stakeholders.

- Communicate some more. Use clarity and confirm understanding.

- Gain agreement and commitment of all parties involved in the change management process.

- Execute the plan, paying attention to what leadership style is required of you to be successful.

- Don't let needed decisions or changes to the plan linger; make the needed calls or convene a group that can.

Leading means eliminating, or at least minimizing, obstacles for the team. Be proactive rather than reactive in your approach.

Stakeholder Analysis

Most situations involving a decision you face in life will be ones where you will be giving something of value to someone or getting something of value from another person, organization, department or group. The entity or entities on the other side of your decision can be defined as a stakeholder in the process. There are usually many stakeholders in career decisions or tasks. By understanding what each stakeholder needs, and aggregating the information on all stakeholders, you can determine how to best navigate a decision toward a positive outcome for all involved.

- Identify the stakeholders. Who has an interest, however minor, in the outcome of your decision or action?

- Evaluate what is important to the other stakeholders in your decision. What is their desired outcome? What pieces of the decision are most important to them?

- What "must haves" need to be addressed directly?

- Can you offer them something of value as a way to facilitate the outcome you want?

- What is important in terms of style or approach?

- What drives a stakeholder's success?

If you take the time to prepare for your conversation or interaction with each stakeholder, you increase the likelihood that you will have a more favorable outcome. Remember, this is equally important in any good relationship in your life—partner, children and friends. Like many skills, once you use this skill regularly it becomes an unconscious capability you simply apply in most situations.

Influencing

In situations where you do not have an ability to say, "Do this" you will need to use some level of influencing to achieve your desired outcome.

- Put yourself in the other person's position and think through his or her perspective.

- Be prepared with your position and be sure to use management by fact as a basis. Facts can be powerful and support your position. Relying solely on advocacy and persuasion may work, but its outcome is less certain.

- Take a personal approach. You need to decide if you are going to be open and engaging, less disclosing and serious, or use a more aggressive posture. You need to consciously send the signal you want through your physical mannerisms and tone of voice. This is also a great parenting skill, especially in the teen years.

- Practice persuasion. Make a compelling argument about the benefits of the outcome. Focus on the broader picture then go into the details needed to get there. If you can agree on a common vision, it will be easier to tackle the pieces. If you can gain agreement on the broader vision, the details tend to get worked out over time.

Keep in mind that influencing will take longer than directing. Issuing a directive does not give permission for dialogue; influencing is based on dialogue.

Influencing is a subtle skill when used right. It comes across as conversational while at the same time you are working towards a desired outcome. It should be viewed as directional rather than absolute. Effective influencing may establish a basis for a future decision; it doesn't have to necessarily result in a decision at that moment.

Negotiating

Negotiating is used when there is a required decision and the parties in the decision need to reach agreement on the key points. People immediately equate a negotiation with a negative connotation regarding tone and atmosphere, but that is not always the case.

The task is to find a compromise that is mutually acceptable to the parties involved. Each party may not get everything he or she wants, but if the final agreement includes some of their top priorities, then it is a success.

There are many times where negotiation takes place in phases, accomplishing a part of the outcome each time. If you are the person negotiating, it is important to be able to detach yourself emotionally so you can think through the process and desired outcomes rationally.

Even within a meeting, there will be times when you will need to mentally step back from the discussion temporarily to gather your thoughts.

Some steps to a successful negotiation are:

- Prioritize what you want as an outcome.

- Determine what you are willing to give in on and what you must have.

- Review your stakeholder analysis and try to make the same list for the other party (parties).

- Effective negotiating gets the desired outcomes without, in many cases, disclosing the prioritization of your key points. Mixing your desired outcomes with areas of unimportance in a negotiation is a nuance skilled negotiators use. Depending on the tone or setting of the negotiation, you will need to present all your outcomes as equally important even though you may only want one or two.

- Understand what the other parties have at stake. Give in, if needed, on points you think are important to them in order to get points that are important to you.

CHAPTER 9

Why Didn't Anybody Tell Me This?

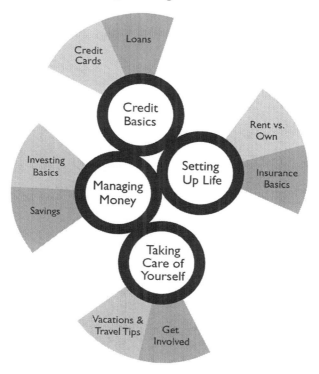

oday's world is filled with extensive choices for managing different aspects of your life. In most conversations about these choices with many of my two adult daughters friends, some common questions emerge. This chapter tries to answer some of them.

Like the skills outlined for career success, these are skills that need to be researched and you should continue a life-long learning process to acquire the knowledge to successfully manage your life. No doubt you will have many more questions about these and other topics. You should seek out resources to get your answers. People, periodicals and experts are good sources, but please ask to avoid the pitfalls of not knowing.

Managing ones financial life is important so that the hard work you put in to earn a living has the most potential to support your lifestyle. Here are a few areas with which to get more familiar.

Credit

Credit broadly is, money someone else will lend to you in exchange for a fee (or return), typically an interest rate. The level of the interest rate is key to understand since it equates to how much extra you are going to pay for borrowing the money.

Do not assume that just because you can borrow the money that you have the ability to pay it back.

The key element to understand about paying interest is that it compounds, meaning it keeps building on top of itself. Yes, you pay interest on what you borrow, but then, next month you pay interest on the interest you got charged last month too! Be aware of the terms of any loan.

Credit cards are enticing. After all, you can have what you want right now by charging rather than waiting until you have the needed funds. Trust me, you will be "profiled" as someone whom the credit card companies want. They look for people who have low earnings, need money and won't be paying them back any time soon. For every $100 you borrow, typically you will pay an additional $9-18 a year in interest.

They only require you to make a minimum payment each month that is very low so the interest keeps adding up and soon you will be deep in debt.

The best general strategy for using credit cards is to only charge what you can pay off each month. Find cards with low rates and, even better, benefits like cash back or points. Use credit cards sparingly for day-to-day items. If you have a larger purchase to make, plan out how you will pay it back to be sure you can afford to put it on the card.

Other forms of credit include loans—student loans, bank loans, car loans, home loans, margin loans. All follow the same interest rate principle.

Be smart in using credit. It can be a powerful way to manage your personal spending, but it has some severe pitfalls when used frivolously.

Investing

The simplest definition of investing is that you use the money you earned to make more money. It would not be possible to put down all the various ways you can invest here because there are almost endless choices. I would strongly urge you to seek out a professional in the field for information before investing yourself.

When you invest money, your expectation is that you receive some form of return, similar to the interest rate concept above except you get paid, rather than having to pay for investing your money.

There is no guaranteed way to make a great return. If there were, almost everyone would use it. Be aware that when investing, there is also a possibility that you may lose money.

You will need to choose whether you think the risks you take are worth the potential gain. Generally, the higher potential returns come with the higher risks of loss. Take the time to understand the potential investment you might make.

One way to start is by saving a little of your pay each month. This will add up over time. Depending on your investment choices and the performance, this savings pool could grow beyond what you put into it.

One great way to begin investing is through a 401(k) or IRA. These are some of the easiest investments to make and usually offer the potential for solid returns. You won't pay tax on the money you save in a 401(k) until you withdraw it later in life. This means your entire contribution will be invested until you retire or take distribution from it. A "company match" is also tax-free. This is a benefit many companies offer to provide an incentive for you to save. Between the investment returns, the match and the tax-free nature of the investment, this savings tool can produce excellent returns for you.

Investments take thousands of forms. Some of the basic forms for you to understand are stock, bond and money market investments.

Stocks are a share of ownership in a company, also known as equity. Stocks are traded on various exchanges and their price is determined by what someone is willing to pay for a share. That price may or may not have a relation to the value of the company.

Bonds are a way to loan money to a company and get an interest rate in return. They are the method a company uses to get credit like that described above. You get paid for loaning them money. Both stocks and bonds fluctuate in price meaning your investment can be worth more or less than you put in it depending on market performance.

Money market funds and bank savings such as CDs were designed not to fluctuate in price and pay a straight interest rate. Because they are designed to have less risk, their payout is lower than bonds.

In general, stocks are the riskiest investments and have the highest *potential* for return; bonds are moderate in their risk and their return is typically less than stocks. Money markets have been the most stable with the lowest return. There are many factors that impact this theoretical framework including the fact that stocks and bonds contain the real risk that they can decrease in value as well as increase.

Typically, one way to decrease your risk is to hire professional help at a low cost by buying a mutual fund. Mutual funds own dozens of positions in most cases and you are paying someone very little to do the homework for you. Costs may be low because they are typically shared by thousands of investors in the larger funds. When you are ready to start investing, call one of the larger fund companies (Vanguard, Fidelity, Schwab, or other similar entities) or a broker for more detailed information and ask your questions.

Other investments will include your home, a car and other tangible assets.

Insurance

You are young and probably think insurance is something you will deal with later in life. Please think again. Insurance protects you from a larger loss that could set you back years in terms of financial savings. Here are a number of areas to consider:

- Medical. It is likely your work can offer you a lower cost option than purchasing health insurance independently, but don't make the mistake of hoping you won't need it. Since rates are low when you are young, get a basic plan that covers illnesses and preventive care.

- Dental. Here you may want to look hard at the plan. Many plans have yearly maximums and will insure costs barely above the total of the premiums. If you have good teeth, you can consider making this an option and buy it only if it is affordable.

- Life. Everyone has an opinion here but if you are single and have no unclaimed children, you may want to postpone buying it. Life insurance pays someone else if you die. Unless you feel like paying someone back for college, you may want to wait until you have financial obligations such as a family. On the other hand, premiums tend to be lower when you are younger and healthier and sometimes, locking in an annual rate should be considered. There are many coverage levels here depending on your age and how much you are willing to pay. Consult a qualified insurance agent to review your options.

- Car. If you drive, get insurance and pay particular attention to the liability limits. If you have an accident and someone is injured, $100,000 can get used up quickly. You can opt for more coverage. One way to keep the premium lower is to increase your deductible to at least $500. The deductible is the amount you will pay first in the event of a claim. Also, bid car insurance competitively as rates change every year.

- Renters or homeowners. Get this. If you have a fire or theft you can get back at least some funds to restock. There are endless "riders" or additional coverage you can buy. Understand the limits that are stated in your policy that outline the maximum the insurance company will pay and buy a "rider" if you have items of greater value. Remember, insurance companies make money by collecting premiums and by figuring out how not to pay claims so understanding the limits and requirements is key. Because the larger name insurance companies may have higher quality ratings they may have more ability to pay, look at them first.

There are other categories of insurance and, if your organization offers them, ask your benefits person for some help. Otherwise find an insurance agent who has been in business a while or call some of the larger companies to discuss your options.

Does Renting Make Sense?

Most people assume renting is cheaper than owning. When all aspects of savings and tax advantages are factored in, sometimes owning can make sense. If borrowing rates are low and you are planning on settling down in an area, take a look at ownership. Owning allows you to build savings through equity in your home and many times is the same cost as renting.

Renting makes sense if you are not sure how long you will live in an area.

- When renting, be sure to read your lease even though it looks daunting. Pay particular attention to any penalties or liabilities outlined in the lease. They show what you are responsible for other than the basics of not burning down the building on purpose, etc.

- Check online for information on the landlord. See if there are any outstanding complaints or legal actions.

- If you rent with other people, understand who is liable. It is usually the person signing the lease so do not be the sole signer of any legal document for another person. This isn't a friendship issue; this is a financial liability issue so don't fall into the "I want to be a good person" trap.

- Don't co-sign anyone else's lease; it is now your responsibility if you do.

Budgeting

While an unpopular and sobering activity, it is worth doing so you can understand how to reach a place where budgeting will no longer be necessary.

Like many other parts of life, you need to have a plan and measure how you are doing against that plan. There are a number of on-line tools that are pretty good like Mint.com and Intuit. Check them out. Failure to plan is simply planning to fail.

Vacation and Travel Tips

Make sure you take time for yourself when you can. Don't leave unused vacation days at the end of the year. They are there to be used and you will be a better worker by finding a good balance in your life. You also risk getting in the habit of not taking your vacation each year and before you know it you have skipped experiences that you cannot retrieve.

The amount of travel you do does correlate to available funds, but don't assume you can't do anything. Life is a set of shared experiences. Experiences can be had at any economic level with some planning.

There are so many "deals" these days that enable you to travel economically. Look at places to travel that are actively attracting tourism through incentives. In addition, the flash sales on airlines are intended to fill seats on short notice for very few dollars. Stay alert and take advantage of the offers.

Alternatively take in what your nearest city has to offer such as walking tours, museums, restaurants. Go to cultural events that are new for you. Use public transportation.

Look for group tours and consider traveling with people you don't know to expand your network.

Keep your passport up to date.

Get Involved

Expand your personal and work world. One great way to do it is to choose a cause and get involved. Schools, community organizations, cultural centers and others all need volunteers to function. Not only can you make meaningful contributions to a cause, you can gain great experience, and even board experience over time. Choose fields you know about or don't know about, depending on your comfort level. They will challenge you to use the skills you are working on and you can actually get valuable practice!

Closing Thoughts

Building a successful career and a meaningful life is something that requires your active involvement. Active involvement means making choices and moving ahead, not waiting for them to be made for you. Finding ways that work for you is part of the process and they must be your choices. You will be the one living with your choices so making ones that fit how you view your place in the world will lead you down your path to success.

Hopefully, what you have seen in this book is that you need more than just knowledge to navigate the path. Being passionate about your continued learning and striving for constant improvement will help you stay focused on moving forward. No doubt there will be some stumbles along the way. Accept those as part of the process. No one gets "everything" right.

If you embrace the idea of learning and improving, new avenues will open for you. You will project yourself in a way that makes both the relationships you currently have, and those you will form later, better.

Start building your skills now. Pick one skill and get good at it, then add another and then another. Remember that there is no one great leap to success. It is usually a progression and progress is not always visible and tangible.

Have confidence the learning process will work for you. I am still a history major just like I was 34 years ago. The difference is I have continued to grow and never stopped looking to add to the skills I have.

There are many factors that will influence your life as you move forward and their importance will increase and decrease during different life stages. Depending on the importance level, you will make your decisions about your choices. Be thoughtful and make the best choices you can and then be supportive of yourself.

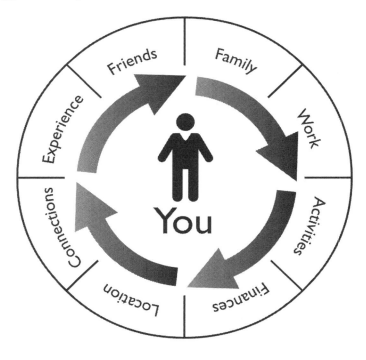

Get started, stay focused and apply yourself and you will improve your competency.

Be strong.
Take charge.
And last but most importantly, HAVE FUN with YOUR life!

About the Author

Christopher Wilson grew up in the Boston area and attended Lake Forest College, graduating in 1979. His mutual career began when he answered a newspaper ad for a customer service representative for Fidelity. Chris worked his way up the corporate ranks for 30 years, becoming the President and CEO of Columbia Funds for Bank of America in 2004. Chris's full career history is available on LinkedIn.

Chris is the father of two daughters, Curry and Talcott, who are both launching their own careers as this book gets published. In 2010, Chris became happily married to his wife Terry, also an author (T.L. Wilson) and public speaker.